# George Kennan

## BOOKS BY JOHN LUKACS

The Great Powers and Eastern Europe

Tocqueville: The European Revolution
and Correspondence with Gobineau (editor)

A History of the Cold War

Decline and Rise of Europe

A New History of the Cold War

Historical Consciousness

The Passing of the Modern Age

A Sketch of the History of Chestnut Hill College, 1924–1974

The Last European War, 1939–1941

1945: Year Zero

Philadelphia: Patricians and Philistines, 1900–1950

Outgrowing Democracy: A History of the
United States in the Twentieth Century

Budapest 1900: A Historical Portrait of a
City and Its Culture

Confessions of an Original Sinner

The Duel: 10 May–31 July; The Eighty-Day
Struggle Between Churchill and Hitler

The End of the Twentieth Century and the End of the Modern Age

Destinations Past

George F. Kennan and the Origins of Containment,
1944–1946: The Kennan-Lukacs Correspondence

The Hitler of History

A Thread of Years

Five Days in London, May 1940

A Student's Guide to the Study of History

At the End of an Age

Churchill: Visionary. Statesman. Historian.

A New Republic

Democracy and Populism: Fear and Hatred

Remembered Past: A John Lukacs Reader

June 1941: Hitler and Stalin

JOHN LUKACS

# George Kennan

A Study of Character

Yale University Press ◆ New Haven and London

Designed by Nancy Ovedovitz and set in Galliard Oldstyle type by Keystone Typesetting, Inc. Printed in the United States of America by Vail-Ballou Press, Binghamton, New York.

Library of Congress Cataloging-in-Publication Data
Lukacs, John, 1924–
George Kennan : a study of character / John Lukacs.
p.  cm.
Includes bibliographical references and index.
ISBN 978-0-300-12221-3 (cloth : alk. paper)
1. Kennan, George F. (George Frost), 1904–2005. 2. Ambassadors — United States — Biography. 3. Scholars — United States — Biography. 4. Historians — United States — Biography. 5. Character — Case studies. 6. United States — Foreign relations — 1945–1989. 7. Cold War. I. Title.
E748.K374L84 2007
327.730092 — dc22
[B]                                                                  2006053107

A catalogue record for this book is available from the British Library.

The paper in this book meets the guidelines for permanence and durability of the Committee on Production Guidelines for Book Longevity of the Council on Library Resources.

10     9     8     7     6     5     4     3     2     1

*To the memory of Stephanie*
*and to the presence of Pamela*

# Contents

Contents

# George Kennan

# ONE

# A Lonely Youth

I

When George Kennan was born, in 1904, there were about eighty-one million Americans. When he died, one hundred and one years later, there were about two hundred and eighty million: so many more, and a different people, and a different country. When this book is published I fear that to the vast majority of Americans his name will be unknown. This is, and will remain, regrettable. He was an extraordinary man, who not only represented but incarnated some of the best and finest traits of American character. Evidences of that make up the substance of this book.

There are great and grave difficulties ahead for his biographers. He was not a celebrity — indeed, nothing like it. He had a very important office in the government of the United States for not more than a few years. The memory and the signification of his name for the diminishing number of people who recognize it exist in their minds mostly because of what he did during those few years. Yes: his achievements at that time — by and large, three or four years in the 1940s — were remarkable. The studies written about him deal with his role during that time. Yet that chapter of his life was brief and transitory. To concentrate on those few years is as insufficient as it is wrong. That is one, but only one, problem that any biographer of his will have to face.

In these few introductory pages I must sketch something of the main course in the life of this extraordinary man. He was but one offspring of the great mass of the American middle classes in the Middle West, a son of a modestly respectable family, not easily distinguishable within that large class of people. There was a dun climate in their lives. George Frost Kennan — there is a coldness in the very middle of his given name, the Frost that he would almost never use, save as an initial. Very soon after he was born his mother died: a loss that constricted this child's heart for very long; his father's choice of a second wife gave little comfort, let alone happiness, to the Kennan children. The young George Kennan was introverted, serious, shy. That temperament marked his personality throughout his life.

He is a student — rather impecunious, and very considerably lonely — he enters Princeton. The interests of his mind begin to cohere. He goes through the entrance examinations of the then recently regulated Foreign Service of the United States. He is posted to various cities in Europe. He marries a young Norwegian woman; they will have four children. He has learned Russian, he knows Russian, he is posted to Moscow: first before the coming of the Second World War, then during the last two years of it. He raises his individual voice — on paper — against the dangers of Russian expansion and Communist aggression. Suddenly — though belatedly — his voice is heard in Washington. He is called home. He is given an important position in the top councils of the government of the United States. He writes an article which rephrases his earlier argument to the effect that it is time to "contain" the Soviet Union. That article becomes and remains the main instrument of his fame. Then he finds that his counsels are wanted less and less, if at all. He resigns.

He does not know — how could he? — that more than a half of a very long life is still ahead of him. Five decades of a mentally active life, seldom interrupted or marred by illness, but inspired by his anxious concerns about his country. He writes great and valuable books, mostly histories, including, at the age of sixty, an unusually fine memoir. He is respected by many but followed by few. He lives and works at Princeton, leading a scholarly and more or less isolated existence, together with his wife. He is almost one hundred years old when he — gradually — puts down his pen. He dies one year and one month and one day after his one hundredth birthday. A long life: blessedly so, not punctuated by great personal crises and dramatic adventures. That may be one problem for a putative biographer.

But there is another problem, or obstacle, which is entirely different and immeasurably greater. It is that the written material he left behind is immense; instead of being too sparse it is too thick; not thin but very rich; not small but enormous in its mass; not in the least insufficient but perhaps even inexhaustible. Such are his literary remains. He was a man of the written word. "The use of letters," Gibbon once wrote, "is the principal circumstance that distinguishes a civilized people from a herd of savages incapable of knowledge and reflection." When Gibbon wrote this, in the eighteenth century, that was a truism, almost too boring to be repeated. But two hundred years later George Kennan's writing — his "use of letters" — had become the principal quality that distinguished him from a herd of otherwise educated people less and less capable of knowledge and reflection.

Sometime around the age of twenty this shy and solitary young student started to write — to write for himself alone. Except perhaps in one instance there was nothing very remarkable about the papers he had to write for his teachers at Princeton. As is the case for most writers, his impulse to write was inseparable from his impulse to read, in his case especially of classics of English literature. That was important enough; but there was more than that. Somerset Maugham said that a young man's "discover[y] that he has a creative urge to write . . . is a mystery as impenetrable as the origin of sex." I do not believe that this is so. Writing, after all, is a form of self-expression. T. S. Eliot understood this better when he said that the motive to write is the desire to vanquish a mental preoccupation by expressing it consciously and clearly. That was the case of George Kennan through eighty years. He wrote to clarify his own mind — and, on occasion, when he so chose, the minds of others. He did not analyze or perhaps even know the source — that is: the motive less than the purpose — of that impulse. He had no desire to psychoanalyze: not himself, and not others.

But he kept writing: diaries, letters, travel journals, notes for himself, through, I repeat, eighty years. This presents an enormous problem for his biographers. The mass of his papers, of his published but, even more, unpublished writings and of his correspondence, is enormous. Historians and biographers customarily struggle against the contrary obstacle: they wish they had more material. In George Kennan's case there is too much. We now live at a time when, for all kinds of reasons, biography is one (and perhaps the only one) form of art that flourishes, since it attracts readers as well as writers. The result is the tendency of biographers to attempt to be encyclopedic, to construct exhaustive or at least nearly exhaustive biographies of their subjects. But what Kennan left behind is not only too much; it is, more than often, too rich. Researchers and eventual authors customarily face the wearisome and often difficult task of reading and reading through reams of papers and other manuscripts buried in archives from which their task is to extract a few sentences that prove or illustrate something. But in Kennan's writings there are passages so well written, so illuminating, that their eventual commentators can hardly paraphrase or improve on them, or not at all.

George Kennan knew that he could compose well and clearly. Did he know that he was an exceptional, perhaps even a great, writer? I do not think so. He had to write — often only for himself, at other times for those close to him. He did not have the desire to be a famous writer. Once or twice in his life he thought of writing a full biography of Anton Chekhov, whom he admired; but even then his impulse was not to become Chekhov's established biographer. He let few people, including members of his family, know that he was writing diaries from time to time. Portions of these he sometimes included in letters directed to family members or close friends. He did not believe that these were extraordinary. He was reluctant when a friend attempted to impress him to collect and publish some of his travel diaries, which he then did, in 1989, under the somewhat indifferent title

*Sketches from a Life.* A last problem, if problem that is. Future students or biographers of George Kennan who wish to know more about psychic circumstances or interior tribulations of his life will learn little about these from all of his accumulated writings. That was not the result of some kind of a Freudian suppression; and it is not attributable simply to Kennan's honest and often severe reserve about himself. That reserve did not exclude or protect him from somber moods of pessimism and even despair: that much we may know. But his interest—and ever so often a profound and penetrating interest—was for the conscious, not for the subconscious, mind: his own and also what he saw of the minds of others. The workings and the evidences and the complexities and the problems of the conscious mind were rich and wide and deep and sufficient for him. So they ought to be for his potential students and eventual biographers.

What is the result of all this? It is that, for the sake of an American posterity, Kennan the writer and thinker is, or should be, even more important than Kennan the political advocate; that Kennan about America is even more important and enduring than Kennan about Russia; that Kennan the actual historian and essayist has left us even more valuable things than Kennan the potential statesman. Though he was often withdrawn and unsure of himself, his character was both more stable and more inspiring than that of Henry Adams. He was a better writer and a better thinker than Adams. The qualities of his achievements were, largely, the results of his mind, of his character, of his conscious employment of his talents. So to the origins and to the formation and to the crystallization of George Kennan's character I must now turn.

2

The American — it has been said and written and declared over and over again — is a self-made man. That may be largely true, but not true enough: because there existed (and, we may hope, there still may exist) significant exceptions (significant, because they are not less American) to that. The self-made man is one whose life and whose career and whose achievements are not determined by his ancestry, by his breeding, by his social provenance. Or, at best, hardly influenced by these; his achievements are largely the results of what he chose to abandon or even reject. A classic American example is Benjamin Franklin, the prime Public Relations man in American history, with his public, rather than private, self.

George Kennan was (and could not have been) more different. He was a deeply private American, who respected and venerated his ancestors. More than that: instinctive elements of his character were formed by his ancestry. In his nineties he paid more and more attention to the history of the Kennans, beyond a purpose to complete their genealogy. That often occurs to and spurs the mind of family fathers after they have reached a certain age. What was unusual was that George Kennan, in his late nineties, chose to approach that kind of work with extensive research and reading and even travel, costing him much expense and effort. The result was a considerable book that he completed in his ninety-seventh year, the composition and the style of which show no symptom of mental decline at that age.

*An American Family: The Kennans, the First Three Generations* is both precise and pensive. The Kennans were people from

Dumfries in Scotland. James Kennan translated himself to America around 1720, and married a New England girl. My purpose here is not genealogy, as it was not George Kennan's either, save where it was necessary to find dates and names. It is to draw attention to a remarkably straight trend. The Kennans were Scots in origin; Presbyterian was the official denomination of their religion. All of them were farmers in small towns, including Thomas Kennan, who served as a Presbyterian minister but returned to private farming after his wife's death. (With him George Kennan's book ends.) They moved, through generations and in stages, gradually westward in New England and then in upstate New York and then eventually to Wisconsin, where George Kennan's grandfather, Thomas, the first professional man, an attorney with a civic reputation* whom George as a child still knew.

Since this book is not an extensive biography but what I hope is a biographical study of George Kennan's character, let me draw attention, necessarily cursory, to four elements in what he obviously received from his ancestors. One of these is physical resemblance: light blue eyes, a strong expressive mouth, self-imposed limits of speech (perhaps, too, repressed emotions of concern and anger), and a large and impressive forehead. The second element is that of personal and family pride or, more precisely, a personal self-sufficiency that George Kennan maintained and possessed throughout this life. People who have written about him emphasized that he, among the "Wise Men" of the late 1940s,† was inhibited because he was bereft of the world-

---

* He was the author of the first published Kennan genealogy in 1907.
† This is the title of the acceptable book written by Walter Isaacson and Evan Thomas, published in 1986, subtitled *Six Friends and the World They Made:* Acheson, Bohlen, Harriman, Kennan, Lovett, McCloy.

wise and wealthy and sophisticated upbringing of his associates and friends. I think that this is insufficient and exaggerated. He was inhibited not because of suppressed feelings but because of his character; he was reserved not because of a sense of inferiority but because of his independent sense of self-esteem.

A third element — expressed again in his family history — is his own, and probably somewhat exaggerated, attribution of the virtues of his ancestors to their New England origins. It is true that the Kennans were not untypical of a large mass of New Englanders who were moving westward and who settled in what later became states and towns and communities in the American Middle West. But did their descendants remain New Englanders for long? Traces of those customs and traditions lived on, but they also became changed, transformed, were even abandoned. I think that, in this instance, George Kennan emphasized the New England factor too much. The true sources of his mind and temperament and inspirations and belonging were broader and deeper than that. It is quite possible that after his retirement from the Foreign Service, Kennan may have found a place not at Princeton but at Harvard. But he would have never become a typical Bostonian. True, New England's remote origins were Scottish and English. The physical and sometimes even intellectual characteristics — and, more important: inspirations — of George Kennan were northern: but also European, meaning, among other things, something wider than Scottish or English or Bostonian. He had what a sensitive French writer in the early twentieth century (it may have been Valéry Larbaud) once phrased as *la nostalgie du Nord,* a phrase whose literal translation in English may be precise but somehow inadequate.

The fourth element that he may have inherited from his

ancestry was something probably not very typical of many of them, and yet something that was a definite component of George Kennan's personality: a kind of sensitivity so fine as to be somehow feminine — surely feminine rather than masculine. It existed not contrary to but in harmony with his other, so often straight and sometimes even rigid but at other times boyish kind of manliness. In his family history, which includes only the histories of the male Kennans, husbands and fathers, he often paused to pay tribute to the women who married them and then bore their children. He saw virtues in them that went beyond the respectable everyday achievements of domesticity. Throughout his life there were some women whom he respected and admired more unreservedly than he did most men.

3

Two months after George Kennan was born (on 16 February 1904) his mother died. His father married another woman who was nervous and cold, a former teacher, not a good stepmother either for her stepson or for her stepdaughters. In sum, George Kennan did not have a happy childhood.

We have seen that his paternal grandfather was the first prominent Kennan. Thomas's son Kossuth Kent Kennan, George's father, born in 1852, was less prominent and a tad less successful, but more learned than was his father: he learned German and French, he was devoted to German music, ranging from Bach to Wagner and Strauss. He was the first Kennan born in Milwaukee, a burgeoning city with its then strong German and democratic influences. His first name was odd because of an episode in American history. Louis Kossuth, the romantic hero and leader of the Hungarian revolution and war of independence in 1848–49, was brought to the United States in 1851 for a whirlwind tour, promoted by politicians and trumpeting publicity, attracting large crowds, the first European who was cheered and thus promoted since the visit of the aged Lafayette in 1824. That flaring (but then soon disappearing) hero worship must have been the inspiration for Thomas Lathrop Kennan to name his son Kossuth. His grandson would dislike that name — probably, too, because later, having learned a good amount of European history, George Kennan had not much taste for romantic and popular revolutionaries such as Kossuth or Garibaldi.

George was an only son: still, the presence of his father did not compensate him for the painful absence of warmth from his stepmother. An intellectual compensation, perhaps: his father had a good library; among other matters, his father also went to Europe often, mostly on business. (He was an eminent student of comparative taxation.) In 1912 he took his entire family to Kassel, Germany, for a few months for that purpose. This had a definite impact on George, who had an early interest in Europe and a talent for languages: at that receptive and impressionable age he learned a fair deal of German fast. But he was not very close to his father.*

There was another Kent, a son born to George's father and

---

* In his *Sketches from a Life* (1989) he called his father "a man whom I must have hurt a thousand times in my boyhood, by inattention, by callousness, by that exaggerated shyness and fear of demonstrativeness which is a form of cowardice and a congenital weakness of the family." He once said that his father, years before his death, summoned him and told him that he could not give any particularly helpful advice to his young son, for he found that the world in which George would grow up was so utterly different from his.

stepmother, whom his mother cosseted at the expense of her stepchildren. This did not pain George, who remained Kent's affectionate half brother through his life. (Kent, a serious professional musicologist, a lonely man, died only a few years before his half brother.) For George, emotional and sentimental and, yes, intellectual compensation was what he received, easily, and with more than usual warmth, from his own sisters: Jeannette, Constance, and Frances — perhaps especially from the first, to whom he would write long letters throughout his life. These young women were quite different: Frances was a rebel, who broke away from her stepmother and chose to be an actress, a bohemian life lived in very different places, from Alaska to New York. It may be a symptom of George Kennan's independence of mind — that exceptional and admirable independence that rose above his otherwise stern convictions and principles — that he loved Frances, respecting and not deploring her rebellious independence. It is not a speculation that it was from and because of his sisters that he received something more than the necessary affection he missed from his stepmother, as well as an inclination toward a feminine fineness of spirit that was one of the — charming — dualities of George Kennan's seemingly (but only seemingly) straight and strict character.

In the first volume of his *Memoirs* Kennan wrote very little about his childhood and early youth — that is: about a large part of his formative years. It may be telling that this volume bears the subtitle *1925–1950,* indicating that this autobiography begins in all seriousness with his twenty-second year, after his graduation from college. To his first seventeen years he devoted only six pages. Yet he had a quick and fertile mind; and many of his private characteristics are discernible before he enters Princeton in the eighteenth year of his life. Writing about them, ever so tersely but also with feeling, he advised the readers of his *Memoirs* of two difficulties. One is, simply, that one cannot remember much of years long ago. The other is "that one moves through life like someone moving with a lantern in a dark woods. A bit of the path ahead is illuminated, and a bit of the path behind" — but not more. I do not quite believe that this is so. I believe, rather, that he did not wish to weary his readers by telling them much about his early youth. Nor do I think that his reason for this reserve was his wish to suppress his memories of an unhappy childhood. Rather, it corresponds to his very conception of an autobiography the essence of which are the lessons, perhaps even more than the successive experiences, of his professional career — with the purpose (for he was inherently a teacher as well as a writer) of telling them something that they ought to know. Whence the odd proportions of these *Memoirs,* I: six pages of his first seventeen years, less than two hundred pages of his first forty years, 1904–44, and then nearly four hundred pages of the following six, 1944–50.

There is, however, almost enough in those few early pages to learn something, suddenly and soon, about one important trait of his character. Next to his, probably exaggerated, excuse of re-calling so little of his early years, comes a telling passage. "There is another difficulty that confronts me when I try to describe my early self. In my youthful consciousness, more, perhaps, than in the case of many others, the borderline between external and internal reality was unfirm. I lived, particularly in childhood but with lessening intensity right on to middle age, in a world that was peculiarly and intimately my own, scarcely to be shared with others or even made plausible to them." There follows a

narration of his acute imagination — imagination, rather than belief, a kind of imagination inseparable from perception — of
fairies and other mysterious beings in a town park, in one instance. That he felt compelled to write almost two pages in that
otherwise so short chapter is telling enough. It is a revelation of
something that few people, except perhaps those who knew him
rather well, understood: and that was the poetic side (side? more
than that, the poetic element) of his mind — something that perceptive readers may glimpse even within the most direct and
concrete examples of his political or historical narratives.

Long before he became "the thin, tense, introverted Princeton
student," as he described himself, we may see many symptoms
of his independence and rebelliousness — for example, "retiring
into sullen rages and sit-down strikes when required to attend
Bournique's dancing school on Saturday afternoons" — but also
on many other occasions. He hated "the grubby military school,"
St. John's,* that his father and stepmother made him attend. His
scholarly record there was unimpressive; he had few close friends
(though in the final yearbook he was recorded as "the class
poet"). More important: the headmaster of that school recognized George Kennan's mental talents; it was he (even more than
George's father) who advised and directed him to apply for admission to Princeton, for the sake of which his loving sister Jeannette helped him to study for the entrance examination.

One more thing about his family and the formation of his
mind. While his relationship with his father was not close, he
respected and loved his father; indeed, he had something like a

---

* Yet he gave a thoughtful and warm-hearted lecture there during his visit to
Milwaukee in 1968.

melancholy insight into his father's character. It was his grand-father, not his father, who, to him, was a prototypical Victorian: the first successful and reputable townsman "who assumed the mannerisms and affectations of the Victorian age, and reveled in them. My father had them, too; but they sat poorly upon him."* This sentence suggests much — among other things, that neither George Kennan nor his father was an American Victorian. At times George Kennan idealized the austere virtues of his remote ancestors of the eighteenth century — while he often thought and said that he was doomed to live in the twentieth. What George Kennan inherited (perhaps from his mother's side — we cannot know) was a romantic imagination, leading, on occasion, to clear and dark premonitions: a temperamental characteristic, seen or known by those who knew him well. But that was not the Emersonian (or Bostonian) categorical duality of emotion as opposed to or against reason; it was, rather, the Pascalian one: his understanding that the heart has reasons that reason knows not — though exist they do.

There was one more, very important, family relation that inevitably enters. George Kennan's grandfather had a cousin, also named George Kennan, who was six years older than George's father. This George Kennan had been the greatest and best American student and scholar and writer about Russia. He lived until 1923, not in Milwaukee but in upstate New York. One day George and his father visited him. It seems that his stepmother did not much enjoy the visit, but that is neither here nor there. What matters is that the visit — the voice and the stories of this old man, and the Russian souvenirs and artifacts in his house — made

* *Memoirs* I, p. 7.

a very strong impression on his young relative, even though it was more than a decade later that, by coincidence, his own life and career became involved with Russia. "Coincidences," Chesterton once wrote, are "spiritual puns." This aphorism is applicable, with something like an astonishing accuracy, to the two George Kennans.* Here I cannot do better than quote the second George Kennan: "The elder George Kennan had no children of his own. In all devotion to the memory of my own father, whose son I recognize myself very much to be — in the sense that I inherited most of his weaknesses if not his virtues — I feel that I was in some strange way destined to carry forward the best I could the work of my distinguished and respected namesake." And that was yet to come.

4

Looking at George Kennan arriving at Princeton in September 1921 we may see a seventeen-year-old boy whose character is largely formed. Looking at him four years later when he leaves Princeton we can see no great change. This does not mean that

---

* "The life of this elder Kennan and my own have shown similarities that give, to me at least, the feeling that we are connected in some curious way by bonds deeper than just our direct kinship. Aside from having the same name, we were, as it happened, born on the same day of the year. Both of us devoted large portions of our adult life on Russia and her problems. We were both expelled from Russia by the Russian governments of our day, at comparable periods of our careers. Both of us founded organizations to assist refugees from Russian despotism. Both wrote and lectured profusely. Both played the guitar. Both owned and loved particular sailboats of similar construction. Both eventually became members of the National Institute of Arts and Letters . . . " Etc., etc.

his four years in Princeton were wasted; but it means that they were less formative than they were in the lives of many of his contemporaries.

He was not happy at Princeton. He knew that instantly. "I was hopelessly and crudely Midwestern." That may have been as others saw him — or, rather, as he thought how others saw him. In any event, he had no compunction to deny such an impression. He had arrived somewhat late, he was the youngest of his class, he found lodging in a rather shabby rooming house, a good geographic and social distance away from the places where his more fortunate classmates were located or situated themselves. Near the end of his first semester there came something sad. He had decided not to ask his father to send him money for a rail ticket to come home at Christmas. Did he have some reason to think that his Princeton enrollment had already cost his father too much? We do not know. To earn some money he took the sole trolley car to Trenton in mid-December, to get a job there as a part-time mail carrier. On his first route, on a snowy and windy day, he slipped on the ice. The assorted mail in his pouch scattered on the sidewalk and in the street; he had the nearly impossible task to gather the letters and to find their now wildly mixed-up destinations. How desolate those December evenings must have been for him, dark nights coming back from Trenton to a rooming house in a Princeton now emptying of students going home for Christmas! By Christmas Eve he had scraped together enough, twenty-eight dollars, the price of a day-coach ticket to Milwaukee. So on Christmas Day he traveled, we may presume, largely alone in a dusty carriage. At home he came down with scarlet fever. He was sequestered in a room on the third floor of their somber house in Milwaukee, bereft of the care and comfort of his older sisters, who had to leave the family house because of the danger of infection. He did not return to Princeton until about Easter; he had lost an entire semester.

After that things became better, but not much. He was not asked to join any of the established dining clubs.* He remained one of the Princetonian lower-class "pariahs." He was tight-lipped and lonely. He had few friends: a cousin, a Catholic intellectual from Kansas (Bernard Gufler) with whom his friendship endured for many years, and another impecunious Princetonian named Missolonghies. The latter and George, perhaps in the wake of their wealthier classmates, chose to spend some of the summer of their junior year in Europe. They sailed on a freighter. Friends as they were, their interests were not entirely compatible. George Kennan was the more serious one; he spent a fair amount of his time in London (at that time he was thinking of becoming a lawyer). They had little money. They ended their grand tour in Genoa, nearly penniless, in search of a cheap berth on an Italian steamship. There George Kennan came down with dysentery, the second of his severe illnesses in three years. He graduated next year.

None of his professors seems to have impressed him very much. This does not mean that he did not gather mental capital during those four years. He was not merely required to but devoted himself to read much, especially in English literature. This connects with a significant episode that he recounted in his *Memoirs*. When he returned after the scarlet fever–ridden months, he

---

* In one instance he — reluctantly — joined one of them but decided to resign after a few months.

absented himself, by and large rebelliously, from one of the required English classes. A young instructor (whose name he could no longer remember) called him in, admonishing him "bluntly but not unkindly." The result: "With all the perverseness of a person of that age, I then repaid his kindness by writing a theme for him, on the subject of what was wrong with the teaching of English in American colleges. When the theme came back with the highest possible grade, I was taught an unforgettable lesson in generosity and restraint. . . . It is not easy for me to picture myself as I was at that time. . . . I see myself, emotionally and personally, as a rather ordinary youth, assailed by very ordinary weaknesses and passions. I was a dreamer, feeble of will, and something of a sissy in personal relations. . . . My greatest assets were a reasonably lucid and open intellect, lazy and passive when left to itself but capable of vigorous reaction when challenged. . . . With this intellect Princeton had done as well as it could, considering the educational conventions of the day."*

Within this honest recollection there is but one caveat that occurs to me. He was not "feeble of will." The independence of his mind lent him a measure of pride that was strong enough to wrestle down much of that sense of inferiority for being and remaining "hopelessly and crudely Midwestern." There is no sign that he wished to emulate or to live up to sophisticated superiors (if that was what they were). Yes: he had something of a romantic vision of Princeton before he went there. He had read F. Scott Fitzgerald's *This Side of Paradise* during his last year in Milwaukee; he remembered that it had affected him rather deeply.

---

*Memoirs* I, pp. 16–17.

Yes: he was, because of his sensitivity, so much more of a Fitz-gerald than of a Hemingway reader and admirer.* But never, through his life, did he show any aspiration to be admitted as a full equal to the company of the rich and powerful, to wealth and worldliness: to the contrary, his demonstrations of reluctance were, at least at times, exaggerated.† He did possess something that was there often during the twenties in the minds (and hearts) of perhaps a myriad of scattered young intelligent mid-westerners who admired and yearned for the, to them, beckon-ing glamour of the cities of the American East—an American version of Englishmen's social aspirations, of the young Evelyn Waugh's kind: but those American aspirations were intellectual (and musical) rather than social. And Princeton in the 1920s was not like the strawberries-and-champagne Oxford of the 1920s, which was all to the good—and for George Kennan, too. How-ever, he remained lonely, and even rebellious, there till the end. He thought that ceremonies were hypocritical and false. "I felt so strongly that when I myself graduated from college, I failed to attend any of my own commencement ceremonies, except the one at which I got my diploma."‡

---

* In his *Memoirs* he wrote that he read *The Great Gatsby* "while still in college. I went away and wept unmanly tears." His memory may or may not have played tricks on him in this instance, for *The Great Gatsby* was not published until 1925.
† The nonconformist radical Humsden, in Charlotte Brontë's *The Professor:* "He prepared to act the real gentleman, having in fact, the kernel of that character under the harsh husk it pleased him to wear by way of mental mackintosh."
‡ Twenty-five years later: "My high principles did not go quite far enough for me to forgo attendance at that particular occasion." In his commence-ment address at Dartmouth, June 1950.

# TWO

# In the Foreign Service

I

George Kennan left Princeton at the age of twenty-one. He was younger than most of his classmates. His grades were average. (His best grade was in history.) He was not at all certain of what he would do, where he would go for a career. In his class year-book the entry for future occupation read: "unknown." He had been thinking of law school, but that impulse weakened. There is some evidence that he thought law school would cost too much. Yet he had, perhaps for the first time, a modest financial leeway: he now got some money which his mother had left him; he needed no longer to depend on his father's support. Immediately after his graduation he took a summer job as a deckhand on a coastal steamer sailing back and forth between Boston and Savannah; he earned little money, but the outdoor work and sea air did him much good. Before signing up on that ship he had decided to give the Foreign Service of the United States a try.

It was a propitious time. In 1925 the Foreign Service, as a possible career, began to attract a fair number of young Americans. In 1924 a long overdue organization of the American Foreign Service took place. The so-called Rogers Act united the previously disparate and politicized Diplomatic and Consular Services, and allowed the newly named Foreign Service to be established on a professional basis, including entrance examinations. Oddly, this act was passed by a Republican president and Congress generally uninterested in foreign affairs and largely isolationist. Yet this institution of an American Foreign Service was a salutary reform with salutary results — until the service became debilitated and liquefied by the enormous inflation of bureaucracy during and after the Second World War.

The time has now come to say something about Kennan's view of the world *aetatis* twenty-one, in 1925. There is a single sentence about this in his *Memoirs* — though, again, a single sentence that says much. "I can recall experiencing, as a fresh college graduate, the prompting of a vague Wilsonian liberalism; a regret that the Senate had rejected American membership in the League of Nations; a belief in laissez-faire economics and the value of competition, and a corresponding aversion to high tariffs." Let us examine this summation. It was not typically Republican: rather, old-fashionedly liberal. Eventually, not many years later, Kennan would no longer espouse a Wilsonian liberalism; he would have few illusions about the efficacy and importance of a League of Nations; and economic questions such as tariffs would be very low, at times even nonexistent, on his mental agenda. But this summation of this young man's view of the world does reflect something that was becoming the *real* division of American views of the world in the 1920s and a decade later: a division between Isolationists and Internationalists, a division that did not really correspond to that between Republicans and Democrats, a division often dividing people within their own parties. In 1925 the large majority of the graduates of Princeton and Yale and Harvard were, or described themselves as, Republicans; but the better minds among them (including those who decided to apply to the Foreign Service) were not isolationists; they were, in one way or another, internationally minded.* So was George Kennan, who did not admire Calvin Coolidge (whom he once saw emerging from the White House to what we now call a photo opportunity, putting on a large Indian headdress of feathers above his sour face).

In September 1925 Kennan took a room in a Washington boarding house. An eccentric and alcoholic but very able old Scotsman ran a private tutoring school for those preparing for the Foreign Service entrance examination. Kennan had a few advantages: his knowledge of history, his acquaintance with Europe, his ability to write, his knowledge of German. Solitary and shy, he was not confident of his ability to succeed in the written and oral examinations. However, he studied hard, took not much part in the social lives of his fellow students and aspirants,

---

* Still: *Isolationism* and *internationalism* are inadequate and imprecise terms — perhaps especially in the case of George Kennan. Soon he found the Wilsonian internationalist idea of Making the World Safe for Democracy illusory and dangerous, as well as the, for him, corrupting belief in American omnipotence, with its temptation of American involvement in any or every corner of the world. But the nationalist and populist isolationism of the twenties repelled him, as it repelled then many sensitive and thinking Americans, because of its shallow belief in Americans as a Chosen People, because of its narrow-mindedness, because of its willful ignorance of the rest of the world.

passed the written test with seventeen others (18 passed out of more than 100), and then the oral one. He was now admitted to the Service, with the requirement to attend its school in September 1926.

Before that he chose to spend most of a summer in Germany, where he read much (including Oswald Spengler) and wherefrom he wrote long letters to his sisters. He now read and spoke and even wrote German almost perfectly. (His interest in German literature and in German history not only remained second to, it was nearly equal to, his interest in matters Russian.) When during the required seven months in the Foreign Service School he was assigned for a few weeks to the Division of Eastern European Affairs, he had not yet begun to learn Russian, but he was planning to do so. In early 1927, soon after his twenty-third birthday, he had his first Foreign Service posting, a temporary assignment at the American consulate in Geneva.

Nineteen-twenty-seven was the peak year in the twenty-year history of the League of Nations, with its prestige at its zenith. Geneva, having shed so much of its Calvinist past, was glittering, and extremely cosmopolitan. Surprisingly, that high electric social and international atmosphere did not discomfort George Kennan. He did not feel at home in Geneva; but he felt at ease. Many years later he recalled that, for the first time, it occurred to him that his position as an official representative of the United States, though no higher than a vice consul, included many tasks worthwhile. That, *pace* George Kennan, was probably more than a surge of self-esteem; it was his satisfaction of being able to properly perform reasonable duties.

There followed his first permanent posting as vice consul in Hamburg. There he felt quite at home. (Throughout his long life

he had an affection for Hamburg.)* He actually enjoyed the
suddenly so multifarious, rather than merely routine, tasks piling
up on the desk and filling the day of a vice consul. In 1928 Hamburg was the largest port city on the continent of Europe, and
George Kennan had a lifelong attraction to seas, especially under
northern skies. Even more than before he wrote and wrote diaries (most of them fortunately preserved). They were the results of his intellectual stimulation while in Hamburg. They were
not a task added to his duties of the day. To the contrary: these
efforts of describing his impressions and experiences lightened
and relieved rather than burdened his mind. It is thus that the
functions of the human mind do not accord with the laws of the
physical world. Whether he knew that we cannot tell. What we
can tell is that during these months in Hamburg he wanted to
learn more and more. He read the, then excellent, German newspapers and periodicals avidly. He went forth in the afternoons
and evenings to attend lectures of many kinds. He was no longer
rebellious; but he was still restless. He thought that his career in
the Foreign Service — a career, even though unusual and interesting, still a bureaucratic one — did not suffice his mind; that he
should reenter some university for graduate studies; he wanted
to know more of the world. He embarked on a long wintry sea
voyage westward across the Atlantic, on a freighter. In Washington he would officially sign off, resigning from the Foreign
Service. The first official he ran into was William Dawson, a

* It seems that between the Geneva and Hamburg postings, while in Washington, he may have courted and perhaps fallen in love with an American
girl whose father was, rather violently, against her engagement to an impecunious young American vice consul. At least for Kennan, good riddance
that was.

former teacher and chief of his in the Foreign Service School. "Like a protecting angel, he intervened to save me from my foolishness."* Dawson advised Kennan that the Foreign Service permitted some of its young members to enroll in a European university for three years of graduate study, for the purpose of special language and area studies. George Kennan chose Russian for his subject, and Berlin for the university. The die — his die — was now cast.

2

What followed now were five years abroad, most of them in eastern and not western Europe. It was still a solitary life, until shared by a wife in his twenty-eighth year. They were five years including changes and many kinds of minor vicissitudes, but beneath and above all that they were marked by another large accumulation of his learning — which was, by and large, what his superiors required. In his case there was much more than that. Those accumulations of studying and learning and writing were not — certainly not primarily — the results of ambition. They were consequences of the inspirations of his mind, rather than aspirations for his career: inspirations to reach out beyond knowledge, to imaginative understanding.

He was fortunate, because the conditions of his career, despite all of its bureaucratic circumscriptions, allowed him to study and

---

*Dawson was one of the high Foreign Service officials who recognized George Kennan's particular talents. Two others were Robert Francis Kelley, chief of the division of Russian and East European Affairs in the Department of State, and William Castle, then assistant secretary of state: erudite Americans of sterling character.

read. He did not feel that then; but he did so later. From the summer of 1928 to the early summer of 1933 he was sent to Berlin and to Tallinn and to Riga, the capitals of Germany, Estonia, Latvia. There were, as yet, no diplomatic or other official relations between the United States and the Soviet Union, then the two largest states of the world.* But that American recognition would one day come. It was beginning to be advocated and promoted not only by Progressives and liberals but by many businessmen too; as so often in American history, great and exaggerated expectations were raised about the prospective economic and financial advantages of trade with a new and enormous state. Independent of such expectations was the reasonable practice of the Foreign Service to support the study of Russia by some of its younger officers, posting some of them in Riga, close to Russia, for the purpose of gathering as much information about the "new" Russia as was possible.†

George Kennan's intense concentration on his Russian studies was outstanding among his then colleages, though not necessarily at the expense of collegiality and of friendships. He was solitary rather than lonesome. (One friendship, lasting through their entire lives, was that with his contemporary and colleague Charles Bohlen.) Whether in Tallinn or Berlin or Riga he kept learning and reading Russian; whenever he could he cultivated personal relations with Russian families who had left

* After 1921 diplomatic relations with the Soviet Union were established, albeit reluctantly, by most governments of the world, except for Switzerland, Yugoslavia, Hungary, and the United States.
† That did not include the gathering of clandestine intelligence: but the Soviets, of course, never believed that. The task of learning Russian and about Russia was a part of their routine consular duties.

their homeland after the Bolshevik revolution. At the same time he read and read German; at times he wrote in German as often as in English. He was not only interested but inspired enough to acquire a feeling for the subtleties of the Russian language, which was no ordinary accomplishment; nor was his intense reading of Russian history and in what may be called classical Russian literature. It was at that time that he first considered writing a biography of Chekhov.

After a few weeks of a temporary assignment in Berlin in 1928, he was sent to Tallinn, where he felt rather alone ("except for the agreeable company of a cocker spaniel"). He moved around the flat Estonian countryside, seeking out the many remnants and the obvious presence of what had belonged to Russia but a decade or so before. After a few months he was transferred to Riga. That was different, and stimulating. Riga was not only larger than Tallinn; it was the most important city and port close to Russia; it was provincial but also quite cosmopolitan, filled with all kinds of people and, more important, chock full of living remnants of older Russian things and once Russian habits and traditions, in places reminiscent of old St. Petersburg, including a nightlife sometimes startlingly so. The weather was gloomy, but often — especially on summer nights — wondrously beautiful. *

---

* Throughout this book I have made a decision to defy the temptation to cite Kennan's own diaries and writings (for reasons that I soon shall attempt at least to suggest); but here, for once, I cannot do so. He wrote about bathing on the Riga seashore "in the nocturnal hours, in the magic and, to me, commandingly erotic twilight of the northern world in the weeks of the summer solstice — the twilight that has given the name to the 'white nights' of St. Petersburg. It was a marvelous, diffuse half-light, marking the unbroken transition of the glow in the northern sky from sunset to sunrise — a condition of nature under the spell of which all human emotions

In the autumn of 1929 he went to Berlin, to enroll in the
University for his studies. He was fairly successful in that en-
deavor. The private sphere of his life extended. He saw much;
but his Berlin was not the feverish, perverse Berlin of Chris-
topher Isherwood. He had a few Russian friends, including a
family whose two sons insisted on accompanying him all the
way one September day to Stettin, where, with his small American car, he embarked on what was perhaps the most important
journey of his life. Most important: because most consequential.
He was sailing to Copenhagen and therefrom to Frederikshavn
in Norway, to marry his bride. She was Annelise Sorensen, a
beautiful Norwegian girl whom he had met in Berlin a few
months before. It was a cold, gloomy passage; in Copenhagen he
had a touch of the grippe; he was uneasy about how her family
would receive him in Norway. He need not have fretted himself.
There was a cozy warmth in that Norwegian house, a warmth
that gave him a sense of belonging to that family for the rest
of his life. Annelise's name occurs but once in his inimitable
*Memoirs.* But she was more than a lovely wife; she soon became
his emotional and intellectual support through many agitations
in numberless times.

They traveled to Vienna on a short honeymoon, and then to
Riga. Their life there turned out not to be easy. Annelise was
pregnant with Grace. They had less money than before, since
Congress had chosen to cut allowances and salaries of Foreign

---

and situations seemed to take on a heightened poignancy, mystery, and
promise." My purpose here is not so much to illustrate George Kennan's
talent to write; it is, rather, to illuminate at least something of the mind
(and heart) of this young American.

Service officers because of the economic depression. Two years later, in the late summer of 1933, Kennan was due to return to Washington. They had to leave the baby with Annelise's family in Norway. Again traversing the Atlantic on a freighter, they arrived a few weeks before Franklin Roosevelt, with the approval of Congress, signed the treaty establishing diplomatic relations with the Soviet Union. Very soon a new chapter in George Kennan's life would open. Those five important years of study and learning were now over.

And now I am facing a problem that any competent biographer of George Kennan must face. At the age of thirty-three his career was not yet impressive. But: he had become a writer of extraordinary talent. He was, and remains, the best and finest American writer about Europe at that time: better and finer than hundreds of others, including Hemingway. This is a strong statement. People, including his admirers, have not yet recognized this. They ought to. American writing about Europe such as Kennan's did not exist before him (and may not exist again). He himself did not know that—which is my problem now. He began chapter 2 of his *Memoirs* ("Training for Russia") by accounting for those five years with a long paragraph explaining and excusing himself: "I find them hard years to write about." Then he admits: "I also wrote quite a bit," mostly descriptions of "landscapes rather than people. . . . They make monotonous and slightly melancholy reading. The reader will, with one exception, be spared them." Well—the reader isn't. Hence the problem. The quality of his prose is extraordinary, his language, his rendering of colors and shapes, of countryscapes and houses, of cloudy climates and city atmospheres, of appearances and expressions of men and women are much more than impressionistic sketches.

They reveal a comprehension that is as high as it is deep, perceptive as well as penetrating, of scenes and places and people, suffused with a knowledge of their pasts, and therefore presenting a historical dimension that cannot exist in the art of a painter, and that is rarely extant in the prose of other writers. So what is there left for any serious biographer than to quote, cite, reprint portions of what Kennan himself wrote? He must have known at least some of that predicament — which is why after thirty years he chose to disinter some of his diaries in order to fill pages of his *Memoirs.** He could not improve on them — and neither can we.

But — fortunately — the scope of this book is limited: a study of character. At this time of his life, still before the age of thirty, his mental — and spiritual — traits are clear and discernible. There was self-doubt ("What is the point of these notes?" he jotted down in Riga in 1932); but there was also self-esteem — or, rather, a rueful but strong assertion of his own mind ("My mental processes will never be understood by anyone else").

He was, among other things, anti-Marxist and anticommunist: but different from the, then and now, usual kind. He was not one of that mass of people whose anticommunism was an ideology popular and populist, containing fears and hatreds — something that Hitler and many people afterward, including in the United States, could and would use to their political advantage, and for a long time too. To other kinds of people communism and Soviet

---

* He devoted less than twenty pages to the first twenty-four years of his life, but then thirty-four pages to the succeeding five years. No less than nine pages, about one-fourth of that entire chapter, consist of portions from his then diaries (plus another two from one of his professional letters to Washington).

Russia in the 1920s and 1930s were interesting, because they seemed something new, and at least one possible alternative to a capitalist order or disorder leaking badly at the time. George Kennan was not tempted by that perspective. His reading of Marx and, even more, his experiences made him see — and astonishingly early — that the so-called class struggle was *not* the main force in history or, indeed, in human nature; that the struggles of nations and of their states were infinitely more important; that nationality was more decisive than class. At the same time he did not dismiss communists with contempt. Watching a demonstration by German communist workers in Hamburg in 1927 he was moved by the somber grimness of many of their faces. In Riga in 1932 he spent long hours conversing with a communist and jotted down notes about that. More important, and more consequential, was his recognition that crystallized even before his first stationing in the Soviet Union: that Russia was, and remained, Russia, communist or not; that, notwithstanding how they were perceived abroad, notwithstanding their ideology and propaganda, notwithstanding their own assertions, the new leaders of Russia were something else than doctrinaire Marxists. Throughout his life, almost till its very end, George Kennan would have plenty of trouble with communist sympathizers but also — perhaps even more — with dogmatic anti-communists of all stripes.

To Hitler's arrival to power in the winter and spring of 1933 he made no mention in his *Memoirs,* and the large catalogues of his papers and diaries and correspondences suggest no reaction. He was in Riga then, and after that in Washington; but he certainly must have read and followed events in Germany with more than desultory interest. Of one thing we may be certain: he knew and understood the weakness and the unpopularity of the Weimar Republic. There was much in the artistic and intellectual life of Weimar Berlin that he appreciated; but he also knew that the parliamentary democracy of the German republic was ramshackle. He thought — and so he would also write later — that the best thing for Germany (and for Europe) after the First World War would have been the acceptance of a constitutional monarchy. But his criticism of, and his impatience with, the small-mindedness of the procedures of democracy went well beyond Germany. In early 1933, still in Riga, he, a minor consular official, wrote and sent a long and thoughtful paper to Washington, where planning for a treaty with the soon to be recognized Soviet Union had begun. In this paper he pointed out, very carefully, how the wording of a German-Soviet treaty of a few years before had failed to assure the protection of foreigners when they were accused of "economic espionage" by the Soviet regime. He then learned that his report, with its warnings, was ignored by the Department of State (and also by President Roosevelt). That was but the first instance of something that vexed him through so many years: the, sometimes fatal, American inclination to ignore or to dismiss or to slur over issues and problems for the sake of leaving public opinion or popular sentiment undisturbed.

Throughout his life he regarded the primacy of domestic politics over the true interests of the state as wrong and immoral. Throughout his life there were many instances for him to lament that condition. But his concern with this predicament went beyond its specifically American phenomena. Well before the thirtieth year of his life, and before his first important (and historically significant) assignment to Moscow, George Kennan became both a visceral and intellectual critic not only of communism but also of liberal democracy. This was something that even his friends and admirers ought not ignore or obscure.

3

In November 1933 Franklin Roosevelt chose William Bullitt to be the first American ambassador to the Soviet Union. A few days after the recognition treaty was signed, someone introduced Kennan to Bullitt, who was immediately impressed, and also with Kennan's knowledge of Russian. Bullitt and Kennan journeyed to Moscow forthwith; the former returning after a few days, leaving the latter to work on the practical establishment of the offices and residences of an American embassy there. Thus for a few months, before the arrival of the embassy staff, Kennan was the principal American official in the Soviet Union. Thereafter he served as regular secretary of the mission.

Bullitt and Kennan appreciated each other from the beginning.* William Christian Bullitt was one of a group of aristocratic Americans (an adjective that I am loath to apply to Americans except in this case, where "upper-class" or "wealthy" will not quite do) who, reacting against the narrow-minded isolationism of Republicans of the Harding and Coolidge and Hoover years, found it natural to gather around Franklin Roosevelt (after all, one of their social class) and offer him their services, especially in the international field: an Astor, a Duke, a Harriman, two Biddles, and Bullitt were among them. Bullitt had had an interesting

---

* Bullitt was thirteen years older than Kennan but predeceased him by thirty-eight years. The last decades of his life were marked by bitterness and solitude.

experience with Lenin and Russian communists fourteen years earlier, after which he was shamelessly disavowed by Wilson, against whom he then bitterly turned; there followed romantic and exciting years, often abroad (he also wrote a novel).* Now he was eager to serve his country again. He was buoyant, worldly, intelligent. His faults were impatience and personal rancors. A few years after Bullitt's death Kennan wrote the thoughtful and warm-hearted Introduction in a volume of his letters that his brother Orville put together and edited.

Kennan lived and worked in Moscow for four years, three of them under Bullitt. They were interrupted by a severe illness, which was treated in Vienna, where the Kennans then remained for many months in 1935. These Moscow years were good rather than bad ones, especially at the outset. There was among the embassy staff an almost exuberant sense of adventure, a comradeship that was intellectual as well as social. Before 1934 the extraordinary privileges which foreign diplomatists could enjoy in Moscow despite their many practical difficulties existed together with easy contacts with Soviet representatives of artistic and intellectual life. After December 1934 that would change. The darkest purge years of Stalin's rule began. Diplomats were now by and large sequestered; their movements were limited. Kennan, alone, attempted to travel back and forth within that vast country, to satisfy, whenever he could, his great and genuine appetite for knowing more and more about Russians, about their remnant traditions, about the presences of the Russian past in their lives. He was sustained by his friendships with his

* I have a chapter about Bullitt in my *Philadelphia: Patricians and Philistines, 1900–1950,* New York, 1981.

colleagues, who appreciated his character and understood the peculiar intensity of his intellect. Charles Bohlen and Loy Henderson were and remained his close friends for life. In other ways so was and remained Bill Bullitt.

All of them saw and felt the dreadful and dark oppression of those Stalinist years. If they had any illusions about the evolution of Soviet Communism, they had abandoned them for good. In one important sense, however, Kennan's views of what was happening were unique. They are there in his diaries, letters, papers, reports. His rejection of communism was of course long-standing; his experiences were not those of disappointment; he had never been anything like a Marxist. But what he saw was that beneath Marxism there was an age-old Russian, here and there even Byzantine, element in the politics of Stalin and of his cohorts: an ancestral suspicion and fear of human differences and of the outside world that explained almost everything of the brutalities and dishonesties of that regime. In a paper ("The War Problem of the Soviet Union") he predicted that the Soviet Union would not ally itself with the West. During a short return to Washington, in May 1938, he gave a lecture to the Foreign Service School, where he said: "We will get nearer to the truth if we abandon for a time the hackneyed question of how far Bolshevism has changed Russia and turn our attention to the question of how far Russia has changed Bolshevism."

He was not quite as impatient as Bullitt, whose expectations of a serviceable American relationship with the Soviet Union turned into a severe disillusion, wherefore he resigned his ambassadorship there in 1936. (Roosevelt now posted him to Paris, where his performance would be exemplary.) Bullitt was succeeded by a multimillionaire, Joseph E. Davies, appointed by Roosevelt, a man who was and remained willfully ignorant of Russia and of the nature of Stalin's government, whose official explanations, including the absurdities of the purge trials, he accepted as proper and reasonable throughout. Soon after Davies's arrival in Moscow the embassy staff gathered and pondered whether they should resign in protest. Of course they decided not to do so.

Well before that Kennan came to see the prospect of American relations with the Soviet Union darkly: "a far cry from the outlook of FDR himself and particularly of those whom he was soon to choose as advisors on policy toward the Soviet Union." We shall see many examples of this. But his solitary estrangement from American politics went wider and deeper than the matter of how to deal with the Soviet Union. In the summer of 1936 he spent a vacation of two months in his ancestral Middle West, in his sister's then home in Illinois (where his wife had preceded him and where their second baby was born) and then in her summer cottage in Wisconsin. Seeking solitude, seeking memories, he chose to retrace one hundred miles in central Wisconsin on a rented bicycle. He felt sad and alone. What he saw (or at least what he thought he saw) was no longer a world of his. He would, because he must, remain loyal to his country. "But it would be a loyalty *despite,* not a loyalty *because,* a loyalty of principle, not of identification." Those emphases are his, written nearly thirty years later, when, again revisiting Wisconsin, he wrote in much of the same vein to his sister Jeannette.*

---

*He blamed much on the automobile. He found a civilization dependent on automobiles deleterious. He remembered one of his professors in Princeton who explained that railroads, coming into the centers of towns, contributed to the growth of an urban civilization, while the asphalt roads extruding from cities lead to their dissolution.

Still—whether "despite" or "because"—there could be no question of his loyalty to the Foreign Service. Loneliness was no excuse for abandonment; and there was, too, a puritanical streak in Kennan's character: a categorical imperative of *duty*. And then, whatever those recurrent black moods and waves of enstrangement, he was and remained a writer, with a writer's impulsive need to subdue his mental preoccupations by expressing them consciously and clearly. That desire, in his case, was self-centered: but it was not selfish. It was inseparable from his—ever growing—inclination to remind people, to instruct them, in his way to teach them.

Here I come to the question of his distaste for democracy that I mentioned earlier: a problem that his biographers must not dismiss or ignore. In some ways it accompanied him throughout his life. In the 1930s his convictions involved more than reforms of democracy; they involved a critique of parliamentarianism and democracy. In 1935, recuperating from his illness in Vienna, he was allowed to work, writing political reports and analyses in the American legation there, led by the excellent American minister George A. Messerschmitt. Austria, at that time, was governed by an authoritarian regime, where parliament and elections were suspended, and political parties, including the Social Democrats and the National Socialists, were suppressed. Kennan approved of that Austrian government. Going further, he believed that their kind of authoritarian government was a healthy and welcome alternative to inefficient parliamentary democracy, as well as to totalitarian police-state dictatorship.* Three years later he began

---

* He was wrong about Austria, where the Catholic and semiauthoritarian regime was not capable of withstanding both the interior appeal and the

writing a book that he then, thank God, abandoned, advocating the gradual reformation of the United States with restrictions not only of immigration but also of universal suffrage. There were too, in both his official papers and private letters, statements critical of Jews and of pro-Jewish pressures (the latter especially in cases of congressmen pressuring immigration cases).* Let me add that in his definite sympathy for certain dictators (such as Mussolini in Italy or Salazar in Portugal) he was not alone; at that time, for example, such were Winston Churchill's inclinations.

In the late summer of 1937 Kennan's posting in Moscow had ended, and he was told to return to Washington for other duties. But there, within the Department of State, another change had occurred. That change was unfortunate, ominous, and perhaps even sinister. It took place a few months after Joseph E. Davies had taken over the American mission in Moscow. The Division of Eastern European Affairs, customarily known as the Russian Division, had been established in 1924 and led by the excellent and studious Robert F. Kelley, who had not only formed that division for the purpose of serious studies but also built up a superb library of Russian materials. In the summer of 1937 it was suddenly abolished, by an executive order, absorbed in a new

---

exterior German pressure of National Socialism — in March 1938 it collapsed in a few hours before Hitler's threats.

* His anti-Semitism was neither general nor categorical. He would cite, approvingly, Germans who said that the sequestration and suppression of Jews impoverished the culture of Berlin permanently. Consider, too, that those were years before the German policy of expelling Jews from Germany changed to the practice of their physical liquidation. Many years later he wrote that what came to be known as the Holocaust was reason enough for the United States to fight the war against Germany.

Division of European Affairs, and reduced to two departmental desk offices, of which only one dealt with Russia. There is some reason to believe that this bureaucratic move was, at least in part, the result of anonymous and procommunist influences of that time. It is significant that Kennan, who, throughout his life, gave little or no credit to conspiracy theories, thought that clandestine influences, together with bureaucratic jealousies and petty intrigues may have been instrumental in that abolition of the Russian Division. He was probably right.

He was now in charge of the small Russian desk for a year, with not much work that was interesting (and with not enough of a salary to live with a wife and two children in Washington). In September 1938 he was sent as first secretary to the American Legation in Prague, capital of the republic of Czechoslovakia, a state that would not exist much longer.

4

Kennan's year in Prague deserves a subchapter in this book. We can see, at that time, some of his startling (in retrospect) prejudices as well as many of his brilliant (and prophetic) insights. Many years later he chose to put a book together about his Prague year. Most of the pages of that book and of the chapter dealing with Prague in his *Memoirs* are filled with his political reporting. He had ample time to do that in Prague. For a future biographer as well as for a serious student of European history of that time they are, I dare to say, invaluable. The "febris" (not "cacoethes") "scribendi" (fever, not itch, of writing) never left him. During his subsequent posting in Berlin he had less time to write because of a steady accumulation of administrative duties.

(There the embassy of the United States, still officially a neutral power, was entrusted with the remnant interests of more and more Western states now at war whose legations had departed from Berlin.) He was also fortunate in working under excellent superiors: like Messerschmitt in Vienna, Wilbur J. Carr in Prague, and then Alexander Kirk in Berlin, who were old-fashioned career ambassadors, men of sterling character.

He landed in Prague at a dramatic moment, on the last regular airplane flight from Paris to Prague, on the day of the Munich Conference. That very day the former Czechoslovakia, as it was then known, virtually ceased to exist. It was virtually abandoned by France and Britain, dictated to surrender a large portion of the country to Hitler, who had threatened (and meant) a European war if the Czechs would choose to resist. They did not. Kennan's mind was well equipped to know what was happening and what would happen. He was not much surprised. Like people throughout the world he was relieved that war did not come. But, again, he was different from the rest. Soon people began to think that the Munich "settlement" was a catastrophe, and not for Czechoslovakia alone: that France (and Britain) should have fulfilled their commitments and not given in to Hitler. Kennan did not think so. In this he differed from many, including Churchill, who was wrong about Munich then (and also later). Churchill was wrong because the French and the British in 1939, with all of their shortcomings, were more ready for war than they were and would have been in 1938: but that is not what should interest us here. What belongs here is the insight and the knowledge of this young American who then and there saw and described at least two fundamental matters about Czechoslovakia in 1938 that were not seen by many otherwise informed people, and that remain generally unrecognized even now. One was that the Soviet Union of Stalin, despite its military alliance with Czechoslovakia and France (signed in 1935) would *not* have moved in accord with those alliances and would *not* have gone to war to defend Czechoslovakia in 1938. The other was that Czechoslovakia was an artificial state, carved out from the old Habsburg monarchy largely according to the wishes of Woodrow Wilson and the French, bound to disintegrate sooner or, at best, later. He knew and thought this, even though he had a sympathy for the Czech people in 1938 and no sympathy for Hitler and National Socialism. His conviction rested on his historical reasoning. He believed that the dismemberment of the Austro-Hungarian Empire after the First World War was an enormous mistake: that the Allies, especially the French, had been grievously wrong in promoting that, and thereafter putting together a series of brittle alliances in central and eastern Europe that turned out to be useless; and that the Czechs and their governments were themselves wrong in building not only their foreign policy but their entire governmental system in accord with that. His reports and letters and remembrances are suffused with his conviction that the Czechs ought to have been more appreciative of what their civilization, including those beautiful remnant buildings and places in Prague and in other Czech cities — owed to the Habsburgs centuries ago. This is but one instance where we may sense the spirit of George Kennan's love and respect for an older Europe, so characteristic of his thinking: musings about history that are more than nostalgic illusions of a past but fundamental perceptions of the then present — a compound of his idealism and his realism.

From the drama of Munich to the drama of Prague (30 September 1938 to 15 March 1939, when Hitler suddenly decided to put a total end to a Czechoslovak state and the German army marched into Prague) Kennan's reports were astonishingly accurate and perceptive. He recognized that the Germans were not quite certain what to do with what was left of Czechoslovakia after Munich, when a Czechoslovak state remained, though necessarily subservient to Germany and hardly independent. At the dramatic early dawn and then through the entire day of 15 March, of which his personal descriptions are, again, inimitable, he saw that Hitler had now taken a step that was a fatal mistake: he had grabbed something that was already largely his, and had given thus the definite impression to the Western world that he was worse than untrustworthy, that he would break his word and make Germany lunge forward where and whenever he so wanted. Even before that day Kennan's indefatigable mind had impelled him to embark on long, solitary drives through Slovakia and Ruthenia, the backward portions of Czechoslovakia. There again, rather accurately, he foresaw that Slovakian nationalism would only profit the Germans, and that (a unique perception then) Ruthenia would have to revert to Hungary. That was indeed what happened. He also saw something that no one else saw then (and the significance of which few historians have recognized ever since). This was that Hitler's tacit consent to let Ruthenia (also called Carpathian Ukraine) go to Hungary was significant, because it indicated that, whether temporarily or not, Hitler now dropped his promotion of Ukrainian nationalism that had been directed against the Soviet Union. We know (or ought to know) that this was but a first step in the direction of an eventual accord between Hitler and Stalin. Kennan did not, as yet, draw that conclusion in March 1939: but when the bombshell news of the Nazi-Soviet Pact burst upon the world five months later, Kennan was one of the few who were not entirely surprised.

Here we must say something about two of his prejudices that marked his mind and even his behavior in Prague—prejudices or, perhaps more precisely, inclinations that he would revise later. One was his skepticism about the viability of the smaller eastern European states and of the characters of their peoples. This varied from country to country and from time to time. His appreciation of Russia and Germany was such that he thought the full independence of many (though not all) of the states between them was, if perhaps regrettably, illusory; and that, more or less consequently, it was not in the interest of the United States to be much concerned with that portion of Europe.* This kind of indifference—a studied indifference, rather than a visceral disdain—is palpable also in his reminiscences, in which he recalled, without regret, how on that tragic Sunday of 15 March 1939 he could not give much, if any, help to the frightened few people, including a Jewish acquaintance, who came to the American legation that morning in despair. He thought it proper and best to turn them out of that building, telling them to go home. That was of course quite in accord with the limitations and the duties of an American Foreign Service officer in those circumstances and at that time. But it reflects something of his character then. Was that side of George Kennan, at the age of thirty-five, callous? No: but it was, self-consciously, cold.

* We shall see that, a decade later, and in quite different circumstances, this was one of the shortcomings of his famous "Containment" article (see pages 89–90)—also that sooner or later some of his ideas regarding eastern Europe changed.

5

At the very beginning of the Second World War, George Kennan was told to proceed from Prague to Berlin and continue his political reporting from there. That may indicate that his talent in reporting was not entirely unrecognized by some in the Department of State, though he continued to think so. His administrative duties in the Berlin embassy were large, but he had (or, rather, he made for himself) enough time and occasion to write. The quality of the written residue of his nearly three years in Berlin and in Germany is as valuable as any. I only wish there were more of it. After all, this was *the* most decisive and dramatic phase of the Second World War, when Hitler's Germany came close to winning it. It may even be said that until December 1941 Berlin was the most important capital in the world. He wrote that, in spite of all of the discomforts and difficulties imposed by the regime and the war, he felt "fairly at home" in Berlin. He knew the city; he knew and understood Germans — as I wrote earlier, as much as he knew and understood Russians. His life and career eventually took a decisive turn after the Second World War because of his reporting from Russia and about Russians, not from Berlin and about Germans. What he thought and wrote during the first two years of that war should be of considerable interest — but only for us, and in retrospect.

He regretted the war; and he pondered his country's role. He deplored what he saw was Franklin Roosevelt's foreign policy, but he knew that it was not a part of his duties to define or assert his opposition to that. And his views of the war were not simple. Did he wish the Third Reich to disappear? and to be defeated? He did. Did he wish Germany to disappear? and the German people to be defeated? He did not. But even this distinction is too simple. He knew that one must not condemn an entire people by identifying everything German with National Socialism; but he also knew that they cannot be seen entirely apart. His view of Hitler and National Socialism was different from that of most people in the Western world, and perhaps especially from the views of Americans. Referring to the title of a then bestseller in the United States, *Germany Sets the Clock Back* (by Edgar Mowrer), he wrote that Hitler and the Nazis were the very opposites of an anachronism; that their ideas and their practices and their instruments were not old and reactionary but new and revolutionary. And Hitler completed a unity of the German people, nation, and state that would remain.

At the same time he was impressed when he saw Germans who remained largely immune to the ideological unity that the Nazis tried to impress on them. He noted this especially in Berlin. There were not a few such instances. He drew on his diaries when he wrote his *Memoirs*. They include nearly four pages of his sitting down with a poor young German prostitute in Hamburg in the early winter of 1939. They reflect a warmheartedness that was as much an element in his character as what otherwise may seem as his cold reasoning. Decades later his German friends recognized that and were grateful for it.

We know little of what went on in his mind in those dazzling weeks and months in the early summer of 1940 when Hitler—and so easily—invaded and conquered western Europe, when it seemed that Germany was winning, if it had not already won, the war. Kennan thought not much of the resolution and the strength of the French and the British before the war. We know nothing of what he may have thought of Churchill in May and

June 1940; most probably he had reservations about Churchill and his rhetoric, though glad for Britain's resistance to Hitler.* On the fourteenth of June the German army marched into Paris. Three days later the collapse of France became an accomplished fact. In those very days the German authorities permitted Kennan to visit, by rail and automobile, the Holland they had occupied; and about two weeks later Paris too.† He thought and thought of what he had seen, and arrived at a conclusion that, again, was unique. He did think that the German domination of Europe could last for a long time. But he also thought that the crude single-mindedness of German nationalism would yield nothing good or even useful for Germany in the long run; that even those who in countries other than Germany were or had become enthusiastic National Socialists would necessarily have

---

* It was much later in the war, in Moscow, when his vision and Churchill's, about the end of the war and what would follow it, began to coincide. In 1944 and 1945 his and Churchill's views were spurned and seen as excessively anti-Russian; then, after 1950, as insufficiently anti-Russian — by many of the same people who had comfortably and profitably adjusted their ideas to prevailing circumstances and to public opinion then, as they had earlier.

† Forty-nine years later, in *Sketches from a Life,* Kennan chose to include long passages from his diaries written during these weeks. Here are but a few words of Kennan about Paris, 3 July 1940: "I struggled all day to find a metaphor for what had happened. Could one not say to the Germans that the spirit of Paris had been too delicate and shy a thing to stand their domination and had melted away before them just as they thought to have it in their grasp? Was there not some Greek myth about the man who tried to ravish the goddess, only to have her turn to stone when he touched her? . . . In short, the Germans had in their embrace the pallid corpse of Paris. They will now perhaps deceive themselves into believing that the city never had a soul. That will be the most comforting conclusion for them to draw."

to sustain their own national interests that would differ from those of the Germans. That of course would happen only in the long run. But even before that: "No people is great enough to establish world hegemony." That single sentence, written in 1940, sums up much — perhaps everything — of George Kennan's view of the world, and of the United States too. Upon that he insisted and thought and spoke and wrote till the farthest end of his life.

In Berlin he was much impressed by the personal character and the views of his ambassador. Alexander Kirk was convinced that the Germans could not win the war. They did not know when and where to stop; and they could not stop. This impressed Kennan. There was another matter for which he was indebted to his ambassador. Kirk had a close relationship with Count Helmuth von Moltke, a Prussian aristocrat, profoundly concerned and bitterly opposed to Hitler's rule and to the entire Nazidom. Kirk, who left Berlin in October 1940, asked Kennan to maintain his contacts and conversations with this great and good man. In Berlin, unlike in Moscow, such contacts, at least at that time, could be kept up, though with a necessary discretion. They left a deep impression on George Kennan.*

In the dark gloomy fall of 1940 Kennan's wife and children returned to the United States. For a long time thereafter Kennan was alone in Berlin. By the spring and early summer of 1941 most remaining members of the American embassy in Berlin could not but sense that a German war against Russia would soon erupt. That came on 22 June, a Sunday. Two days later Kennan wrote a long letter to his friend Loy Henderson, who had the important

---

* He had another contact with another Prussian nobleman, grandson of Bismarck. Helmuth von Moltke was hanged before the end of the war.

post in the State Department dealing with Russian and eastern European affairs. He preserved Kennan's letter, the gist of which was: "Never — neither then nor at any later date — did I consider the Soviet Union a fit ally or associate, actual or potential, for [the United States]." He would cite this sentence in some of his later writings. He also wrote: "I feel strongly that we should do nothing at home to make it appear that we are following the course Churchill seems to have entered upon in extending moral support to the Russian cause in the present Russian-German conflict." "Material aid wherever called for by our own self-interest," where needed: yes. But treating the Soviet Union as an ally: no. For Kennan that was a moral imperative. For once, Kennan was wrong. Churchill, whose contempt for communists and communism was even stronger than Kennan's, saw things clearer and better throughout the war (indeed, even in 1939, when Stalin chose to join Hitler). There were only two alternatives: either all of Europe dominated by Germany, or the eastern half of Europe dominated by Russia; and half of Europe was better than none. For once, Kennan's realism was wanting. The problem was not merely American shortsightedness, and Franklin Roosevelt's apparent and evident expectations about Stalin and the Soviet Union. It was an illusion to think that American and British material aid to Russia at war could exist together with a refusal to include Russia as a partner in the war. After all, Hitler's Germany proved to be strong enough not to be conquered by one, or even two, of its great imperial enemies: not Britain, not America, not Russia could defeat Germany alone; not Britain and America, not Britain and Russia; all three of them had to conquer Hitler and his Reich.

Kennan, in Berlin, was now very lonely. He would not see his

wife and children for nearly two years. Such separations of families were often unavoidable conditions during the careers of
Foreign Service officers. The dark nights of wartime Berlin, experiencing the first air raids by the British, only contributed to
his gloominess.* In December 1941, then, came the news of
Pearl Harbor and the German declaration of war on the United
States. That was of course expectable and expected. There now
followed five difficult months when the remaining American
colony in Germany were interned in a hotel in Bad Nauheim
until they would be released in exchange for German officials
returning to Germany from Washington. Kennan was now in
charge of a group of about one hundred and thirty men, women,
and children, the behavior and the demands of some of whom
exasperated him. (The food allotted to them was severely re-
stricted, but other conditions of their internment were acceptable.) Except for his occasional impatience with some people, his
leadership during this internment was admirable: his characteristic talents came to the surface; he took it upon himself, for instance, to entertain them with serious lectures, including topics

* In a letter to his wife, 21 October 1941: "In general, life in Berlin has been
much as you knew it. The major change has been the wearing of the star by
the Jews. [This had been decreed one month earlier.] That is a fantastically
barbaric thing. I shall never forget the faces of people in the subway with the
great yellow star sewed onto their overcoats, standing, not daring to sit
down or to brush against anybody, staring straight ahead of them with eyes
like terrified beasts — nor the sight of little children running around with
those badges sewn on them. As far as I could see, the mass of the public was
shocked and troubled by the measure, and such demonstrations as were
provoked were mostly ones of friendliness and consideration for the vic-
tims. Probably as a result of this fact, the remaining Jews are now being
deported in large batches, and very few more stars are to be seen."

of Russia. He was their leader; and — a self-imposed task that he would, perhaps not too consciously, attempt to fulfill so often during the rest of his life — their teacher, too.

He was — with ample reasons — vexed with the lassitude and the relative indifference with which the bureaucracy of the Department of State treated the matter of their internment. Then that came to an end; and, via Spain and Portugal, he and the internees sailed homeward across a sunny Atlantic in early June.

Concluding this subchapter I think I must, once more, sum up something about George Kennan and Germany. He often remembered (and in his *Memoirs* found it proper to recall) the words which Hitler's foreign minister and toady Ribbentrop threw at the American chargé, Leland Morris, summoned to the German Foreign Ministry to receive the German declaration: "Your President wanted this war; now he has it!" There is reason to believe that George Kennan, utterly different from and contemptuous of someone like Ribbentrop, found these words, alas, to be true. He did not agree with Roosevelt's and his government's inclinations and politics regarding Germany, as he did not agree with their expectations about Russia. We shall see when and how and why he expressed this during the war; he did some of the same, on occasion, about their treatment of Germany, too. His understanding for the people of Germany equaled his understanding for the people (of course not for the government) of Russia. He believed that an unduly harsh treatment of Germans immediately after the war was wrong; that the policy of categorical "de-Nazification" was wrong; that the Nuremberg war crimes trials were wrong. It was not until 1947 that American official policy toward Germany as well as toward Russia changed: the former independent of what Kennan had written and proposed, the second promoted by and in accord with Kennan — but, as we shall see, not entirely, and not for long.

6

When in June 1942 George Kennan returned to the United States, he was given a well-deserved two months of vacation. He and his wife looked around and bought a farm in southeastern Pennsylvania, a wise decision; this became their second (and sometimes first) home almost till the end of his life. Moreover: after 1942 those unavoidable separations of this Foreign Service officer on duty from his wife and family would now occur less and less frequently and for shorter periods. It was fortunate, for instance, that Kennan's wife was permitted to follow him after he was again posted to Moscow in 1944. Before that he was assigned to two important posts: Lisbon and London.

In Lisbon he became the head of the American embassy, since the ambassador had suddenly died, less than a year after Kennan's arrival. He had two important duties in Lisbon. One was that of sensitive and clandestine intelligence. The other involved the American purpose to acquire bases on the Portuguese islands of the Azores, in the mid-Atlantic. On the westernmost edge of Europe, Lisbon was a neutral state, well situated as its gate to the Atlantic, and ever since 1939 filled with many kinds of intelligence services, agents, and clandestine professional or amateur missions, including representatives of states allied with Germany but hoping to abandon that tie and, with that purpose, gain some hearing and potential support from the Western Allies, especially from the United States. We have few records of Kennan's contacts with them, but they did exist, and gave him further insights into the complicated (and later, tragic) destinies of certain eastern European states.

More important was the matter of the Azores. Washington approached it clumsily and badly. Kennan was enraged by that. There is no need here to describe, even briefly, those complications, except to note that his mind remained exercised by them for many years. In the end the Gordian knot (if that was what it was) was cut by a debonair slash of the sword by President Roosevelt himself, who received and heard out this young Foreign Service officer.

Three convictions crystallized in Kennan's mind during this time. "Crystallized" may not be the best word, since they had existed in his mind well before: but now they became acute. One of them was his anger at the bureaucratic incompetence of the State Department: they issued directives that were untimely, unreasonable, often senseless. Another vexation, increasing rapidly at that time, was the supine subordination of the (otherwise inflated) department to the imperious requirements of the even more rapidly burgeoning American military machine, whose representatives abroad often made Kennan despair because of what he saw as their ignorance. And then there was his estimation of his president. That, too, was not new in 1943: he had had his reservations about FDR's statesmanship and, perhaps, about the president's very character before. Now, when Roosevelt instantly, and "with a debonair wave of his cigarette holder," cut the Portuguese knot by telling Kennan to ignore everybody else: that he would write a personal letter to Doctor Salazar, Kennan was relieved and grateful. Yet even that did not change his view of the statesmanship of the leader of his country. (He had, we may presume, a higher estimation of Portugal's leader, Salazar.)

In January 1944 Kennan was sent to London, to represent the United States in the European Advisory Commission, a body then instituted for designing the military zoning of Germany at the end of the war. Again there were conflicting directives that vexed him; again, for a few days, he had to return to Washington and see the president himself. Beyond the matter of the drawing of the zonal boundaries in agreement with the British and the Russian representatives of the EAC, Kennan was much concerned with what he saw as the attitude of Washington and of the White House about Germany, with their belief that some kind of a satisfactory accord could be reached with the Russians about the status of Germany and the treatment of the Germans at the end of the war. He wrote two long memoranda about this, one to a colleague in Washington in 1943, the other to the American ambassador in London in the spring of 1944. Neither of these, he thought, was read by high officials responsible for America's German policy and plans at the time. Perhaps not. Perhaps, even if so, his warnings may have had no results at all. Yet it seems that his pessimism may have been exaggerated. His opinions may have been unpopular or untimely, but his character began to be respected by not a few people whose influence did count.

7

George Kennan and Charles (Chip) Bohlen had become close friends in Moscow during the thirties. Their backgrounds and temperaments and personalities were different, their views and opinions also differed on occasion, but they respected and liked each other. Their friendship was an example of the condition that the essence of true friendship between men is almost always intellectual: a genuine appreciation of a friend's mental and spiritual, rather than of his physical or material qualities. Bohlen was instrumental in establishing Kennan's assignment to Moscow in 1944 — the assignment that turned out to be the most decisive in his career.

Now the American ambassador to Moscow was Averell Harriman, a confidant of Franklin Roosevelt. There was a vacancy in the embassy; Harriman was in need of a minister-counselor, in charge of many matters, second in rank to him. Bohlen advanced Kennan's name to Harriman (and perhaps also to Roosevelt). Harriman was impressed with Kennan's qualifications and of course with his knowledge of Russian. Bohlen arranged a dinner with Harriman and Kennan; the position was then offered, and Kennan of course took it. That occurred after Kennan had come down in London with a bad ulcer and, back in Washington, had been granted a blessed five weeks to recuperate at his farm. He thought that the Department of State did not quite know what to do with him. That was not so. Bohlen had spoken to Harriman about Kennan even before the latter's return from London. What was typical of Kennan was that during their informal dinner he took it upon himself to say that his views about the Soviet Union were not necessarily those now held by the Roosevelt administration. He and Bohlen took a long walk after the dinner, arguing with each other.

It seems that Bohlen had judiciously told Harriman what to expect from Kennan. It is to Harriman's credit that he would bring Kennan to Moscow, no matter what. The evolution of their relations does credit to both of them. Their personalities were quite different. Harriman was an American multimillionaire, an impressive and handsome man, not intellectual but more than superficially sophisticated, knowledgeable of men and women and of much of the world. Kennan was more intellectual than wordly: that much we know. In 1944, besides differences in temperament and character, there was a difference in their respective views of the world war and of the Soviet Union. Harriman had a broader view of American-Russian relations than had Kennan. He knew how much the United States *needed* Russia in the war. Consequently his perspective was closer to Roosevelt's than to Kennan's: he thought that the fact of the wartime alliance was more important than all other problems due to the nature of the Soviet government, and that there had to be cooperation between the United States and the Soviet Union lasting not only throughout the war but also after it. Harriman knew that Kennan did not think so. Whether he read Kennan's papers and memoranda that Kennan began to draft almost from the very instant he arrived in Moscow we cannot tell. I am inclined to think that Harriman did not willfully ignore them, but that he inclined to put them aside, perhaps for the time being. About six or, at most, eight months after Kennan's arrival in Moscow, gradually, slowly, Harriman began to see and to interpret the accumulating evidences of Soviet behavior and of Soviet ambitions more and more as did Kennan; and another six months later there was no longer any great difference between their views.

It was in late June 1944 that Kennan started his journey to Moscow. That was a long and arduous trip, via Portugal, Italy, North Africa, and the Middle East. The relentless heat took much out of Kennan.* The speed of air travel notwithstanding it took him two weeks to get from Italy to Russia. Once in Moscow, he began to contemplate and to write about what he was seeing almost immediately.

He thought that his mind was open; that, perhaps, the wartime alliance with the United States and Britain, all of what that entailed, may have changed the regime of the Soviet Union enough to be different from those dark years of the late 1930s. But he quickly concluded that this was not so, and that to believe or trust in a friendly Soviet Union was now not only a useless illusion but a danger involving the very interests of the United States.

He, as so often, was beset with the sense of loneliness. Coming to the embassy he met a staff of new people, none of whom he knew when he had left Moscow seven years before. He thought that they reacted (if they reacted at all) to his opinions with "bored insensitivity." We may, again, have reasons to believe that this was an exaggeration. But, in any event, it contributed — and to our benefit, enduringly — to the feverish energy with which he devoted himself to move around as much as he could and to write and write — to put down on paper, almost instantly, a vast amount of his impressions, and thoughts. That of course was his habit through most of his life. But it may be that he has never written as much as during the first half-year after his return to Russia. It all began with his diary writing. Less than a week after

---

*His diary descriptions of those horrid days and nights are superb. At the time of this writing it may be of interest to read his scathing views about Baghdad and Iraq on pages 184–85 of the *Memoirs,* I.

landing in Moscow he was out and about, trying to travel around Moscow and the surrounding countryside as much as was possible. After less than ten days in Moscow he spent an entire Sunday traveling, as he hoped, incognito, on a crowded suburban train, trying to see and hear, listening to people, and speaking with some of them. His diaries cover pages and pages about his impressions on that suburban excursion. A few days later he felt compelled to record his long conversation with a Russian acquaintance, a government official, a conversation that was remarkable because this Russian, for once quite openly, dismissed Kennan's complaints about the rigid limitations with which otherwise sympathetic foreign observers, such as he, were forced to be isolated from Russian natives of all sorts. And then this Russian added that there was another reason to watch out. Russia was now winning the war. She was victorious; and foreigners ought to be especially careful when that happens: for at such a time it is natural for Russians to be brutally confident of their own strength; different to deal with than when they are down and out and in need of foreign support. Another few days later Kennan stood on a broad Moscow pavement, watching the forces marching past of perhaps fifty thousand German soldiers, an endless mass of stumbling prisoners of war, a parade obviously mounted by the highest Soviet autorities to impress the people of Moscow. George Kennan's heart was full of sorrow and sympathy for these, mostly young, Germans: again he thought that an entire nation cannot and should not be condemned; I venture to write that he would have agreed with Edmund Burke: "People, Sir, must never be regarded as incurable."

He was now in Moscow at the very time, in a month that may have been most crucial for the future of Europe: August 1944.

The defeat of Hitler's Germany was now certain. The liberation of Western Europe, of almost all of France and of Paris, was proceeding rapidly. In eastern Europe the Russian armies had now reconquered almost the entire territory of the Soviet Union before the war; they were moving ahead in the middle of Poland and about to enter southeastern Europe, where (against Churchill's wishes) there would be no British or American military presence. What would this Russian preponderance in eastern Europe mean? That was not a primary concern for Washington (it was more of a concern for Churchill in London); but it was a primary concern in George Kennan's mind. And even before the massive Russian surge into the Balkans (and Hungary), the main issue was now Poland; and he had a front-row seat to watch and consider what was going on, there and then.

There were two grave questions about Poland. One: what shall be the shape of a new Poland after the war; the second: how would Poland be ruled, and by whom? The first of these questions was already tacitly and largely agreed upon by Roosevelt, Churchill, and Stalin at their Teheran summit conference, months before; the second had now become more important and acute. Less than a month after Kennan's arrival in Moscow came two ominous events, decisions by Stalin, the full importance of which Kennan recognized at once. One (on 29 July) was the Soviet announcement of the formation of a Polish committee in Lublin, behind the advancing front of the Russian armies, composed mostly of procommunists and communists, rather obviously the kernel of a future government of all of Poland. The other was Stalin's decision to halt the Russian armies but a few miles before Warsaw, where the so-called Home Army, the Polish underground, had risen (on 1 August) in a heroic struggle to force the

Germans out of Warsaw. There *was* a legal Polish government exiled in London, much more than a shadow congregation of political émigrés, having raised, among other achievements, one hundred thousand Polish soldiers and airmen fighting alongside British armies almost everywhere. In 1941 Stalin felt compelled to recognize that government; but in 1943 he broke Russia's relations with them. Now, in July 1944, there was a faint possibility of a combination of the London and Lublin aggregations, agreeable to Stalin; Kennan was in the middle of that, both as an American official in Moscow and an observer. He did not say much; but he was convinced that the free Polish regime, in London, was doomed. And then his indignation, at times amounting to suppressed anger, arose at seeing the almost incredibly rigid and callous Russian behavior during the Warsaw Rising. Obviously Stalin did not want to see Warsaw rescued and liberated by the Polish Home Army alone;* let the Germans and the Poles kill each other — that may be best for Russia.

At that very time George Kennan concluded — and he came back to this conclusion many years and decades later — that August 1944 was the moment when the Western Allies should have confronted Stalin and the Russians with the demand that they define their objectives in eastern Europe. Kennan was probably right about this. He was certainly right about the need to seek some kind of agreement about Russia's postwar ambitions, to nail them down, if possible, sooner rather than later. He was perfectly right in seeing that the American concern with Russia's behavior in eastern Europe one or two or three years after the

---

* Which, one must admit, was the unspoken political objective of the Rising.

war amounted to locking the barn door when the horses were gone. His analyses written at the time were farsighted, their best features due to his customary realism. He wrote that the main issue was not communism: what Stalin wanted were people, not always necessarily communists, but people entirely subservient to Moscow. There were two other, incisive and penetrating, elements in Kennan's diagnosis of the Russian-Polish problem. Again one was historical, not ideological. Looking back at Russia's treatment of Poland one hundred and thirty years before, he saw its recurrence. Then, too, a tsar and his government did not wholly absorb Poland within the Russian state; but sooner or later it became evident that these Russian concessions and promises meant nothing; Poland was to become a subservient annex to Russia. The other element that Kennan thought worth considering was psychological, issuing from his extraordinary insight into some of the old and odd vagaries of Russian souls. In 1940, whether directly or not on Stalin's orders, the Russian secret police had murdered more than four thousand captured Polish officers in one fell swoop, in the forest of Katyn. Kennan thought that at least one of the reasons why Stalin would not allow an independent or semi-independent Polish regime to exist was that there must be no mention of Katyn: after all, brutality carries a wake of suspicion and guilt; and, in the case of Russians, perhaps particularly so.

About that, too, Kennan was — more than probably — right. Yet we must note something like a contradiction between his then preoccupation with Poland and his larger view of eastern Europe. Before 1944, and for many years afterward, too, he believed that America's vital interests did not include eastern Europe; that the United States must not approve what happens and what would happen in eastern Europe; that the interests of America (and Britain) were to the west of that portion of the continent. He foresaw that the Russian subjugation of eastern Europe was now well nigh unavoidable; and that therefore Washington should eschew any kind of American statement about that. In this he was probably mistaken, since such expressions of American indifference about eastern Europe (or indeed about almost anywhere else in the world) would not only have been impossible because of public opinion but would only have encouraged the Russians to proceed without any limitations whatsoever. But then Kennan still thought — and almost always correctly — in terms of geography and history, including spheres of interest: we must not approve but consider Russia's interpretation of her own spheres of interest, just as Russia must comprehend the interests of the United States in its neighborhood, in the Caribbean and South America and the Pacific.

There was another matter about which Kennan was largely right. This involved the then congealing mass of American expectations for a new and fundamental international order, established by a supernational institution such as the United Nations. He was not involved in the preliminary planning of that; but he was concerned that those expectations could and would obstruct and obscure the primary problem of American relations with Russia. He foresaw, accurately, that fateful American concessions would be made in order to assure the Soviet Union's entry into the United Nations; that this concentration on that target would mean the simultaneous neglect of dealing with problems that seemed less attractive but were, in reality, more important. Then, and thereafter, Kennan's interest in the United Nations was skeptical and limited. And this brings us to one of his most telling papers or memoranda, thirty-five pages long, entitled "Russia—Seven Years Later." Many years afterward Kennan ranked it as better and more important than his famous "X" or "Containment" article in 1947. More consequential than the "X" article it was not; but more telling, yes. Such is not only the irony of history but also the fate of all kinds of writing, including masterpieces.

And a masterpiece "Russia—Seven Years Later" was: a profound and, here and there, brilliant analysis and description of Russia's material and economic and domestic and cultural and intellectual and political and spiritual conditions and evident tendencies: how and what these were, and what could (and what could not) be expected from them. For once, he wrote this study—more than a survey, a veritable essay—not for himself alone: he gave it to his ambassador, who then read it, said little, and sent it on to Washington. Here again was one facet of George Kennan's aspirations and talents, together with those of a writer and historian: that of a teacher. For the unwritten and unspoken subtitle of "Russia—Seven Years Later" may well have been: "For the education of Mr. Harriman about Russia." More than sixty years after the essay's composition this historian will but note one of Kennan's stunning insights about realities that are even now far from being recognized by most historians. For the sake of an example, his conclusion of what had really happened during the purges of the 1930s was that "the ship of state had been cut loose from the bonds of Communist dogma"; that Stalin was a limitless autocrat, a peasant tsar, and not an international revolutionary. (Alas, even some of the best and most honest historians of the Russian purges attribute Stalin's brutalities to his having been an extreme dogmatic Marxist.)

Kennan did not know whether his ambassador found the time and the inclination to read these thirty-five or more pages; but it seems that Harriman did. More than thirty years later Kennan wrote: "I often think: what a trial I must have been to him, running around with my head in the usual clouds of philosophical speculation, full of interests other than my work . . . bombarding him with bundles of purple prose on matters which, as I am sure he thought, it was the business of the President to think about, not mine — and all this when there was detailed, immediate work to be done." Readers: this kind of superb modesty is not an oxymoron. It belongs here, too, because Kennan's and Harriman's appreciations of each other were now accumulating.*

8

The year 1945 was a great, perhaps the greatest, turning point in the history of the twentieth century. It was the end of the Second World War; indeed, the end of the era of great world wars; it was the end of the second, and last, German attempt to dominate Europe; it was the year of the first two atomic bombs; it was the end of the Japanese empire, and of many other things besides; it was the year when the division of Europe, and of Germany, and of Berlin began. It was also a year of a slow

---

*He wrote about Harriman: "His integrity in the performance of his duties was monumental and unchallengeable. . . . The United States has never has a more faithful public servant. . . . I, in any case, can do no other than record my gratitude to him — for his patience with me, for what he taught me, for the example he set." Patience and good manners are of course not unrelated to wisdom.

turning around of American-Russian relations, a prelude to a coming cold war, and to the definition of American policy for it two years later.

But 1945 was not a turning point in George Kennan's life — not yet. Throughout that year his habitual pessimism remained unbroken. Clouds of dark despondency crowded his mind. Again he saw, from many evidences, often day after day, that his admonitions against the shallowness of American expectations about Russia were unheard, unnoticed, unread. The only satisfactory development was the now increasing inclination of his ambassador to see things no longer very differently from him; yet even that did not mean that Harriman agreed with Kennan about everything; also in 1945 Harriman was away from Moscow for weeks, sometimes for months. Kennan's mental health was sustained by two things. One was the presence of his wife and children: Annelise Kennan was a pillar of stability and of good sense, capable of restraining her husband's frequent moods of severe pessimism. The other element was his compulsive habit of writing — even when thinking that he was writing for himself alone.

He was not included in the preparations and in the management of the Yalta and San Francisco and Potsdam conferences. That he minded not at all: he was skeptical of their importance and dismissive of many of their results. We have seen that he was, rightly, critical of the American (and neo-Wilsonian) belief that a new international institution such as the United Nations was of paramount importance, perhaps the crowning result of the Allied victory of the war. He knew the limitations and the often senselessness of general declarations of agreements with Moscow. Beyond that, his knowledge of history and his understanding of human nature were sufficient to sustain his basic conviction that national and state interests were and would remain more powerful than any international organization dedicated to assure some kind of an unchanging peace.

Was his — at times overwhelming — pessimism warranted? Yes and no. There *was* a rather definite change in President Truman's attitude toward Russia compared with President Roosevelt's: but Kennan attributed little or no importance to this at that time. It was true that this new president's solid character was such that only a few days after his assumption of his office in the White House he found it proper to speak sharply to the visiting Molotov; but it is also true that the next day he relented somewhat, and that throughout the remaining eight months of 1945 and to some extent even into 1946 Harry Truman did not abandon the American policy of hoping that some kind of a reasonable and enduring relationship must and could yet be achieved with Stalin's Russia. We know that this was not how Kennan saw the immediate future. Very telling is his bitter criticism of the political habits of his own country with which his diaires are filled through 1945, considerable portions of which he found proper to reproduce in his *Memoirs* more than thirty years later. For a few months in 1945 a slew of American political personages, former and present ambassadors, senators, and congressmen, flew into Moscow. Stalin received almost all of them. Kennan was appalled by their overall ignorance, by the shallowness of their interests, often by their very behavior. One of the few exceptions to that was Harry Hopkins, whom Truman sent to see Stalin at the end of May. Hopkins had met Kennan before and respected him. When Kennan told Hopkins that he saw not the slightest hope of influencing, let alone changing, Stalin's treatment of Poland, Hopkins listened and understood what Kennan meant, but both he and Kennan knew that just about nothing could be done. These august American visitors chatting and smiling with Molotov and Stalin included men who less than a year or two later turned out to be violent, dogmatic, and anticommunists. "General" Patrick Hurley, traveling via Moscow to become American ambassador to China, shocked the entire staff of the embassy as he approved (and reported to Washington) every assurance that Molotov gave him about Russia's benevolence toward China. One of the appalled officials was John Paton Davies, the China expert in the embassy. A few years later Hurley attacked this man viciously, accusing him of communist sympathies and affiliations. (Kennan stepped forward to defend Davies.) Then there was General Eisenhower's triumphal visit to Moscow in August, the general grinning broadly and embracing General Zhukov, toasting American-Soviet friendship. Less than eight years later he was president, telling Americans that any kind of agreement with Russia was useless (and telling Churchill that Russia was "a whore").*

Toward the end of 1945 the course of the giant American ship of state began to show its first slight but nonetheless indicative changes; but Kennan's gloomy days and nights in Moscow persisted. He was deeply aware of the American tendency to wholly

---

* Well before that time (1953) Kennan would see, and experience, that the worst American illusions about Russia in 1945 and before were no more damaging — and no more contemptible — than the dogmatic denial of any consideration of Russia, at a time when ideological anticommunism became not only an element of but a virtual substitution for American patriotism.

subordinate foreign policy to domestic political advantages. A typical case was the Moscow visit of James F. Byrnes, now the secretary of state, Kennan's immediate superior. Harry Truman, for political reasons, had chosen Byrnes to be the secretary after the hapless Edward Stettinius. Kennan was not the only one to foresee that the Moscow Conference of Foreign Ministers in December 1945 was bound to lead nowhere. Still, he was shocked by Byrnes's carelessness. He saw through him, recognizing that Byrnes's main (and perhaps only) aim was to return to Washington with some kind of agreement, no matter how meaningless and immaterial; and that Molotov and Stalin understood that only too well. Kennan thought that serious conflicts between the United States and the Soviet Union were bound to come — but that his country and its people were unprepared for that.

He was the acting head of the embassy when, on the morning of the Russians' own announcement of V-E, Victory in Europe day, there rose a mass demonstration of the people of Moscow facing the embassy building, unexpected and unprecedented in the history of the Soviet Union. It was a spontaneous and enormous wave of popular gratitude for how much America had helped Russia during the war. There was a strong sentimental strain in Kennan's character; but during that unforgettable day his mood was somber. He knew that this outburst of Russian popular sentiment did not accord with what the government felt and thought; and that it would not last. But his profound affection for the people (and for the country) of Russia remained enduring. One of his few pleasant experiences in 1945 came when he could visit some Russian places far from Moscow, where he could talk with all kinds of Russians. At the same time

he understood, and sometimes emphasized, strange and unpleasant traits of Russian character that were age-old national traits
and not attributable to communism.*

In 1945 George Kennan was a Cassandra, a visionary and a
prophet, unheard by his country. What one hundred and fifty
years before Charles James Fox had said about his great opponent Edmund Burke applied to Kennan: "a wise man; but . . . a
wise man too soon." However, there were two aspects in Kennan's then view of the world that were insufficiently realistic. He
did not recognize how important it was for the United States
that the Soviet Union should enter the war against Japan — a
commitment that Stalin gave to Roosevelt and fulfilled. But then
Kennan's main interest and preoccupations always concerned
Europe and not the Far East. He believed, for moral as well as
for practical reasons, that the United States could and therefore
should do and say nothing about eastern Europe; that such pro-
nouncements as the Yalta "Declaration of Liberated Europe"
were deplorable, sham and useless, because eastern Europe was
now Stalin's sphere of interest. Oddly, or perhaps not so oddly,
Stalin thought much of the same. His interpretation of Yalta and
of that pallid grandiloquent declaration was that Roosevelt tacitly understood the practical state of affairs: "What is ours is ours;
what is theirs is theirs" (Stalin's own words later). This was so:
the division of Europe was the unavoidable result of the Second
World War. Yet was it at all possible to keep a tight-lipped silence,

---

*This view (and realization) differed from those of interpreters of Russia
who wrote about "the new Soviet man" (such as the Webbs and even E. H.
Carr); but also from anticommunists (such as Alexander Solzhenitsyn)
who declared that Lenin's and Stalin's rule was an utterly alien yoke forced
upon the Russian people.

a tacit acquiescence in that division? In this democratic age was it possible for governments to publicly state their indifference to what was going on behind what would be Stalin's iron curtain? And so it was eastern Europe — or, more precisely: American expressions of concern over what was happening in this now Russian-ruled portion of Europe — that worried and impressed Stalin. What was happening in eastern Europe led to the beginning of the so-called Cold War.

In 1945 Kennan was more concerned with Germany than with eastern Europe. He foresaw, well before the Potsdam Conference, that there would and could be no agreement between America, Britain, and Russia about what would happen with Germany. The best and most practical way was to accept a division of Germany, and begin the rebuilding of a free Germany in its western half, unoccupied by the Russians. That was the gist of a long paper, entitled "Russia's International Position at the Close of the War with Germany," that he wrote in May 1945 and gave to Harriman. (He did not believe that it would be read in Washington; yet there is some evidence that Hopkins read it.) This was yet another excellent paper or, rather, essay from his pen. I wish only to draw attention to one of his most startling and prophetic observations. One of them was that communism and Marxism were gone, outdated. "Pure Marxism is dated; and if its flame still animates to any appreciable degree the power of the Kremlin (which is questionable) . . . the fire of revolutionary Marxism has definitely died out. What remains is capable of inspiring patriotism and nationalist sentiment, both for defense and for imperialist aggrandizement." The second — perhaps even more telling for our purposes — was his prediction that the Russians' power over eastern Europe would not be long-lasting.

"Russia will probably not be able to maintain its hold success-fully for any length of time over *all* the territory over which it has today staked out a claim. In that case, the lines would have to be withdrawn *somewhat.*" These italics were his. Somewhere else in that essay he also used the adjective "indigestible." He could not know that Churchill had used that very same term when speak-ing about eastern Europe to General de Gaulle a few months before.* There was, too, a masterful description of Stalin in this paper, including, here and there, Kennan's sober recognition of at least some greatness in him.†

But, after all this was said — and written — in the winter of 1945–46 Kennan again felt and thought himself hopelessly alone. After Byrnes's useless visit to Moscow he sat down to write yet another paper: a practical instruction for Americans on how to deal, how to treat, how to speak with Russian officials: a kind of Teacher's Guide that he never sent. His mood had again darkened to an extent that, for the first time in many years, he thought that he might as well resign.

---

* In November 1944. "Russia is now a hungry wolf in the midst of sheep. But after the meal comes the digestion period."
† La Rochefoucauld, *Maxims:* "There are evil men in this world who would be less dangerous if they had not something good in them."

# THREE

# First Officer on the Bridge of the Ship of State

I

Alone in the Moscow embassy (Harriman was, again, away for some weeks), Kennan was ill. It was February 1946. Bedridden, but bound to deal with a mass of routine matters, he read a routine telegram from the Department of State, transmitting a query from the Department of the Treasury. It dealt with the Soviet government's disinclination to agree to the standard American proposals of adherence to the World Bank and International Monetary Fund. What could their reasons be: what did the Russians really want? Kennan's reaction to this inquiry was anger. Here was another, lamentably ignorant, query about how and why the Russians were the way they were. Worse: it came from the Treasury Department, whose top personnel and whose views, especially regarding Russia (and also Germany) were notable for their — not always innocent — naïveté. Kennan first thought to respond to their query with a curt answer, a kind of dismissal. Then, ruminating in his sickbed, he began to change his mind. Here at least was another chance to draft yet another serious memorandum, in this case a summation of how and why the regime of the Soviet Union behaved and could be expected to behave. This query by the Treasury people was but an excuse, a potential instrument for such an explanation, even if it should be read by hardly anyone beyond the Russian desk at State. Kennan rang Dorothy Hessman, his excellent secretary, and dictated the — later so famous — Long Telegram of eight thousand words, from his bed.

History — and a man's life — is full of unintended consequences. "Unintended consequences," rather than "answered prayers" — because Kennan expected not much from this "elaborate pedagogical effort" (as he later put it). For him it was but one self-imposed task of serious writing, impelled by a sense of duty but also by yet another impulse to clear his own mind. And then the effect of the Long Telegram was rapid and sensational. It arrived in Washington on a holiday, Washington's birthday, 22 February. Soon it was circulated, reproduced, sent and read by the secretaries of war and navy and, it seems, by President Truman himself. Historians came to regard it, rightly, as one of the principal documents and instruments of the change of American policy toward the Soviet Union, indeed, of the beginning of the Cold War, an importance comparable to Winston Churchill's Iron Curtain speech a month later, and to the Truman Doctrine, to the Marshall Plan, to Kennan's own containment "X" article a year later.

It certainly impressed the minds of those in charge of the course of the American ship of state. It instantly changed the course of George Kennan's life. "My reputation was made. My voice now carried," he wrote some thirty years later. "My official loneliness came in fact to an end—at least for a period of two to three years." His official loneliness, yes; his personal loneliness: yes and no. It is both interesting—and revealing—what he thought of this sudden and dramatic turn of his life. Yes and no: because he was both pleased and saddened as he saw what was happening. We know this from what follows the story of the Long Telegram in a long paragraph in his *Memoirs:* a serious analysis of how ideas move and travel—especially in Washington.* He was not a man who gave in to the obvious temptation of saying to people: "I told you so."† But he was more than

* "Six months earlier this message would probably have been received in the Department of State with raised eyebrows and lips pursed in disapproval. Six months later, it would probably have sounded redundant, a sort of preaching to the convinced. This was true despite the fact that the realities which it described were ones that had existed, substantially unchanged, for about a decade, and would continue to exist for more than a half-decade longer. All this only goes to show that more important than the observable nature of external reality, when it comes to the determination of Washington's view of the world, is the subjective state of readiness on the part of Washington's view of the world, is the subjective state of readiness on the part of Washington officialdom to recognize this or that feature of it. This is certainly natural; perhaps it is unavoidable. But it does raise the question—and it is a question which was to plague me increasingly over the course of ensuing years—whether a government so constituted should deceive itself into believing that it is capable of conducting a mature, consistent, and discriminating foreign policy. Increasingly, with the years, my answer would tend to be in the negative."

† Perhaps to some extent in his *Memoirs,* whence its Annexes, reprinting the entirety or parts of four of his crucial papers in 1944 and 1946.

irritated — he was pained to see how so much of the result of what one says or writes depends on timing, that is, on the actual, rather than potential, willingness of people to read or hear. After all, he thought, the Long Telegram was not much more than a strong restatement of what was, or should have been, obvious. He was, in retrospect, not entirely pleased with it. There was too much in it about communism, rather than about age-old Russia, about ideology, rather than about history and geography. That emphasis, and the very success of its receptivity, would vex him again and again. So many people would see him now as an Expert of Communism, even more (or, rather) than an expert on Russia.

2

So now we arrive at the most decisive and best known four years of George Kennan's career: 1946 to 1950, when he was summoned to stand on the bridge of the American ship of state, one of its highest officers, close to the table charting its course, subordinate only to a few men. Attempts to survey these four years may be either too easy or too difficult. Too easy: because the main story is, or at least ought to be, rather well known. Too difficult: because the mass of documents wherefrom something like a precise reconstruction of the plenitude of those days and years could be composed is enormous. However — this book is not an extensive biography but a study of character. That, too, is not easy: because there are dualities in the character of every human being, and because there were, or at least seemed to be, contradictions in Kennan's own opinions during these years. Yet there was a consistency of his convictions, enduring as they were, more essential than the seemingly — and often only seemingly — contradictory expressions of his opinions on occasion.

The quest for recognition is almost always the result of loneliness. Kennan was a lonely man; yet public recognition did not much attract him. And now his sequestered life in Moscow would be followed by the swirl and whirl of Washington, enforced silence succeeded by inevitable din. All of it came rather suddenly. Three months after the Long Telegram he and his family were in Washington. The first task assigned to him came even earlier. He was to help organize and give lectures to the new National War College, to the most promising young officers from the various armed services of the United States. His was a new office and title: deputy for foreign affairs. He threw himself into this task with enthusiasm. He was not to be disappointed. He found most of his officer students commendably serious and intelligent. He was in high spirits for the time being. He was sustained by another self-imposed task: building his family homestead. He, his wife, and his children were now able to devote weekends to rebuilding and improving and planting their house and garden and farm near East Berlin, Pennsylvania, about two hours away from Washington. He began writing a Farm Diary. He had a sentimental view of the virtues and pleasures of country life (for him those pleasures were always agricultural, not squirearchical); the work was difficult and endless, which he did not mind. Then came a second assignment. He had little experience in public speaking; but somehow anxious people in the Department of State must have recognized his capacity as a kind of teacher, to educate select American audiences about the Soviet Union, and of the consequent necessity of confronting Soviet ambitions if and when required. They sent him off to a speaking tour.

There his experiences were not as gratifying as those at the National War College. Here we ought to keep in mind that in the development of American-Soviet relations, indeed in that of the American view of the world after the Second World War, 1946 was a transitional year. On the highest levels of government the realization that the time had come for the United States to resist and respond to evidences of communist and Soviet aggressive ambitions had begun; but even then there was, as yet, no definite plan of where and what must be done. And then in 1946 American public opinion was still inchoate as well as divided. The wartime illusions and ideological inclinations to give so many benefits of doubt to the Soviet Union were still prevalent. As in so many instances of American history, there was a divergence between public opinion and popular sentiment. Though here and there overlapping, the two were not the same: much of public opinion was still reluctant to jettison optimistic hopes about international order and the Soviet Union, while evidences of popular sentiment suggested a growing animosity against the latter. The audiences selected by the Department of State for the purpose of hearing Kennan were composed of potential representatives of public, rather than of popular, opinion. He spoke to more than half a dozen such audiences. They differed. He found, especially when he spoke to academic audiences, including those of top atomic scientists in California, a deadening incapacity to think at all realistically about the world as it was, together with a cramped and dishonest unwillingness to rethink, let alone abandon, their progressive ideas about the Soviet Union. Kennan thought that not only communist sympathizers but active Communist Party members existed among some of these university audiences, noting and reporting what he said. Yet — and this is the first time that I must draw attention to this important condition—even then he thought and said that the extent of communist influences within the United States ought not be exaggerated.* A few months later, in another speech at the University of Virginia: "I deplore the hysterical sort of anticommunism which, it seems to me, is gaining currency in our country." So it was.

After the speeches sponsored and arranged by the Department of State in the summer, came more and more demands for lectures. His energy astounds. He seldom would repeat a speech or lecture; he kept up his habit of dictating or writing their texts, on the average of five thousand words each. At the same time he went on with his lectures and other duties at the National War College. Their qualities impressed his listeners, some of them recalling his phrases many years thereafter. He was gratified by their reactions. So were his superiors in Washington. Here was an exceptionally useful spokesman for the government, at a time when public opinion had to be prepared for a turn in the course of the giant American ship of state. Thus in 1946, for once, he was in sync with the high governmental mindset in Washington. (For once: because soon thereafter this would not be so.)

Then came the real turning point in 1947. The new course was set: and the Cold War began. Nineteen forty-seven was to be the highest point in George Kennan's public career—though not his life.†

---

*Twenty years later he wrote: "The penetration of the American governmental services by members or agents (conscious or otherwise) of the American Communist Party in the 1930s was not a figment of the imagination. It really existed; and it assumed proportions which, while never overwhelming, were also not trivial."

† We now see that his "annus mirabilis" was 1946, not 1947.

3

Things began early enough. By January 1947 General George Catlett Marshall had accepted the office of the secretary of state. Dean Acheson was his undersecretary. Both of them knew Kennan now. Marshall was convinced of the necessity for establishing something of a high-quality planning staff in the Department of State. The excellent and intelligent General Walter Bedell Smith had suggested Kennan to Marshall for the head of such a group. Marshall told Acheson to contact Kennan, without as yet committing himself. Then, on 24 February, Acheson called Kennan to his office, telling him to come that evening to a meeting for a special committee that would have to discuss a grave problem that had arisen. The problem — or, rather, a challenge — was that of the decision of the British Labour government to relinquish its military and financial commitments to Greece, where something like a civil war was going on between the royalist democratic government and a communist armed insurgency. It should be recalled that for many years Greece had been a problem for the British alone, who in 1944–45 had sent forces into Athens to defeat a communist uprising — for this they were then sharply attacked by American opinion and criticized by the State Department itself.* But now a British government, beset with all kinds of material troubles and in the process of dismantling many of Britain's former imperial commitments and presences, turned to the United States: would the latter assume a responsibility for

* It should also be remembered that Stalin at that time did nothing, absolutely nothing, to help the communists in Greece or even to criticize the British. That was consequent to an agreement he had made with Churchill in October 1944 in Moscow (the so-called Percentages Agreement).

Greece, to take on the effort of supporting it against the threat of its local communists? That night the unanimous opinion of the committee, including Kennan's, was: yes, that was what the United States must and should do.

Unanimous as that "yes" was, resounding it was not. Members of that committee were impressed by the directness and the clarity of Kennan's remarks. But what Kennan did not know was that a decision had already been developing, if not altogether taken, by the president and his advisers. What was to be called the Truman Doctrine — and that *was* a definite turning point, more than just a milestone, in the history of the United States — was already in a state of being born. There was no question of, or time for, an abortion, or even a Caesarean section. The main problem, for the president and the highest circles of his government, was now its delivery: its packaging, for the purpose of its acceptance by Congress (and by that often nebulous mass that goes under the imprecise name of public opinion). Ten days after that memorable meeting on 24 February, Kennan realized this. On 6 March he was shown the draft of the paper that another six days later President Truman would read to the Congress. It disconcerted him considerably. He spoke of his reservations to his friend Loy Henderson and to Dean Acheson. They listened to him, but his criticism had no effect. The Rubicon would be crossed, and the American people and the world would hear the terms and phrases that soon came to be known and are still known as the Truman Doctrine.

There were two reasons for Kennan's unhappiness with the text — and, implicitly, with the meaning — of the Truman Doctrine. One was its, to him, entirely unnecessary pairing of Greece with Turkey. There was no communist guerrilla or underground activity in Turkey. Defeating a communist insurgency in Greece would be a sufficient contribution to the security of Turkey. His other caveat, not unconnected with the first, was the universal and sweeping phrasing of the president's message that announced an American commitment to support (and, by tacit assumption, militarily) any people threatened by "armed minorities or by outside pressures." Kennan thought not only that such a universal, or nearly universal, commitment was unnecessary but that it would carry the definition of America's national interests too far, eventually even astray.*

Here was the first of many instances where George Kennan and Dean Acheson did not agree. Their characters and their provenance were different. It may not be an exaggeration to say that Acheson regarded Kennan as too intellectual, even at the cost of a necessary pragmatism, and therefore often impractical. This is not to say that Acheson did not have a considerable respect for Kennan — or that the former did not deserve to become a secretary of state (with qualities well above those who would succeed him during the next fifty or more years). But their relations were not close. Also — Acheson's opinions and his views of the world were more changeable than were Kennan's. As late as 1946 Acheson was still looking for possibilities of

---

* It may be interesting to notice that in some of his discussions, especially with the National War College students and study groups, he said that even a communist victory in Greece would not necessarily benefit the Soviet Union: another example of his clear and steady distinction between the threats of communism and of Russian interests. At the same time he was unconditional and steadfast in his conviction that there was now an American challenge in Greece which could and should be met — and with relative ease and relatively little cost.

accommodation with the Soviet Union. But by March 1947 he thought it both politic and proper to "sell" the Truman Doctrine to Congress with a — wholly exaggerated — language in order to frighten its members with the prospect of a Red tide sweeping all over western Europe unless the present administration took a stand — in Greece and Turkey this time.* A decade later Acheson attacked Kennan's then propositions for some kind of a mutual disengagement in Europe; another five years later he was one of the most vocal hawks among those whose advice was solicited by John Kennedy during the Cuban missile crisis. But I am running ahead of my story, the essence of which is how early George Kennan learned, or had to learn, that his influence in helping to chart the course of American foreign policy was quite limited even when his official position was high. In any event, both Acheson and he could see, in 1947, how American popular sentiment and public opinion were changing: for instance, how former extreme isolationists became radical interventionists, for whom no American move against the Soviet Union could be drastic enough.

Kennan's relationship with General Marshall was quite different. Marshall liked Kennan from the beginning of his acquaintance with him. His esteem for Kennan was more than considerable. Kennan admired Marshall's character unreservedly; not for a moment did he rankle or fret being Marshall's subordinate. There were occasions when he was awed by Marshall's tight-lipped rectitude; there were others when he was at first stunned

* All of this did not protect Acheson later from most contemptible attacks against him from many Republicans and then from Joseph McCarthy for being "soft" on Communism.

and then amused by the general's abrupt rejoinders (as when he once reproved Kennan for putting the ice in glasses before the whiskey). Marshall had Kennan occupy the very office in the State Department building next to his. Nothing more than a door separated them there — an easy access of which Kennan took as little advantage as he deemed possible.

Important, for our purposes, is Kennan's role in the making of the Marshall Plan. This has been often obscured by historians' and political scientists' cconcentration on "Containment," the "X" article. But Kennan's contribution to the Marshall Plan must not be neglected. General Marshall returned from Moscow to Washington on 20 April 1947. He called in Kennan the very next day, telling him to gather a Policy Planning Staff immediately — if that meant that Kennan had to drop his job at the War College for the remaining semester, so be it. Kennan put his staff together in less than ten days. He thought that he could do this without relinquishing his last lectures at the War College; nor did he cancel two or three other lecture engagements to which he had felt committed. What future biographers should note was not only his amazing energy but that he was an author — or, perhaps, even *the* author — of the Marshall Plan. The drafts that he, as head of the Policy Planning Staff, presented to Marshall were approved, at times entire paragraphs — all this after Marshall (and, on occasion, Acheson) had studied their wording minutely. The Marshall Plan amounted to a promise of instant (and generous) American material and financial aid for the purpose of restoring the economies and stabilizing the societies of western European states. The aim was political and social, not military: to diminish whatever danger may have existed of communism there taking advantage of desperation or chaos.

Kennan took little or no credit for this stellar achievement. That was due to his character. We must of course consider that he did not work alone. Long hours were spent together with his small staff, listening and arguing: one evening, exhausted, he walked out to a corridor and burst into tears. But there were no profound or personal disagreements muddying the drafts of final texts; and, after all, he was their chief of staff. However, some interest is due his speech at the War College on 6 May 1947. Note that he prepared this speech less than five days after Marshall had summoned him to establish the Policy Planning Staff; five days within which they had their first meetings, in addition to his other speaking engagements. It is my opinion that his 6 May 1947 speech is at least as significant as the Long Telegram or as the "Containment" article. It contained a most judicious, and telling, summary of his convictions about the Marshall Plan and beyond. In one sense it was too pessimistic. He said that, after swallowing eastern Europe, and with the existence of strong Communist Parties in western Europe, the Russians may "feel . . . that Europe is in reality theirs, although Europe may not know it." That was not so; and it contradicted his own convictions, expressed not only later but suggested elsewhere also at that time, that the Russians would have sufficient trouble to digest the portion of Europe that they were now swallowing. But those above-cited words about Europe were not the essence of his thesis, masterfully developed in that speech. Material conditions, the economies of the nations of western Europe, must be improved, soon, with American help. And Europe, especially western Europe, was more important — not only for the interests of the United States but for civilization in its entirety — than other parts of the world. And within Europe, the status of West

Germany (and also of Austria) were especially important. The time had arrived, finally, to dispense all expectations for reaching agreements about Germany together with the Soviets. The recovery and the strengthening of western Europe was now a prime, and urgent, American task.

All of this corresponded with the Policy Planning Staff's (and, in this case, largely Kennan's) completed draft of the Marshall Plan, presented and approved by the secretary of state on 23 May and pronounced by him at his now famous address at Harvard on 5 June. But there were also other elements in Kennan's War College speech that are worth considering. As in the case of his propositions about Germany, he suggested the recognition of the military and political status quo: concentrate on the western part of Germany and on the western part of Europe. Yet at the same time Kennan argued (and General Marshall adopted this in his address and thereafter) that such a plan for the American-assisted recovery of Europe should include the entire continent. It should be offered even to the Russians — even though they would probably not accept it. The emphasis must be on Europe; and the Truman Doctrine must not be considered as a universal American commitment everywhere on the globe.

It may be proper, at this point, to say something about Kennan and Europe. Here was a quintessential American, of a midwestern provenance, with an ancestry whose origins were Scottish, far away from continental Europe: a man who was critical of earlier American interventions in Europe, who had clear and strong ideas about the limits of America's national interests, who — in some ways and on some occasions — could be seen as an isolationist. But such a designation could not but be misleading. From his early youth Kennan had an intellectual and even spiritual respect for Europe — especially for Old Europe. Many of his phrases and arguments in his abovementioned papers and speeches reflected this. He did not, unlike others, argue only about the necessity for an economic reconstruction of western Europe, or how such a material effort would accord with America's own interests. At least on one occasion he, at least implicitly, suggested that America owed something to nations (and not only the English-speaking ones) in that part of Europe that originated and shared some of America's own traditions. Such a conviction marked not only his political but also intellectual interests throughout his life. Still, at least in 1947, there was an innate contradiction there. Europe, yes: but which Europe? On one level Kennan's mind accepted the division of Europe. The Russians now had eastern Europe; alas there was not much to be done there. It was a sufficient task to contain them behind that "iron curtain"; for the United States to commit itself to the recovery and defense of western Europe. On another level of his mind he thought that the division of Europe (and of Germany) was a grave misfortune, the disastrous consequence of the Second World War, and that it should not last. This was more than an intellectual desideratum. He thought that such an unnatural division of Europe would not and could not endure; that sooner or later the Russians would have to retreat, at least somewhat, from their now acquired domains.* But that insight he did not

---

* In this, as in many other matters, Kennan's views of Europe were similar to Churchill's. Both were accused of being unduly anti-Soviet in 1945; both would be accused of being unduly willing to negotiate with Russia in 1953 and after. They were seen — wrongly and shortsightedly — as inconsistent. Yet there was a stunning consistency in both Kennan's and Churchill's views of Europe before, throughout, and after the war.

express or suggest within the "Containment" article and doctrine, to which we must now turn.

The origins of the "Containment" or "X" article are easy to trace. There was another high official in Washington who respected, indeed admired, Kennan: the secretary of the navy, James Forrestal. (It seems that in February 1946 Forrestal was mainly responsible for the immediate circulation of the Long Telegram at the highest levels.) He was a self-made man, strong-minded, agitated by his convictions about the dangers of the Soviet Union and of communism and communists, hardly separable in his mind.* In December 1946 he and his staff prepared a long paper about this important topic. He gave it to Kennan to read. Kennan agreed with much of it but had a few qualifications. Man of the written word as he was, he wrote a long answer to it a month later. Forrestal liked that and, again, began to circulate Kennan's paper here and there. Around the same time Kennan was invited to address the Council of Foreign Relations in New York. He responded to this with little difficulty. For once, he spoke without a written text, with the reminder of a few notes; his mind was still replete with what he had written in response to the Forrestal paper. Then Hamilton Fish Armstrong, the highly respected and excellent editor of *Foreign Affairs,* the journal of the Council of Foreign Relations, asked Kennan whether he could publish there a written text of Kennan's remarks. Kennan, properly, requested official permission to submit the text (which was almost identical with his paper written to Forrestal)

---

* His unstable temperament, together with the extreme agitations of his mind, led to his tragic suicide in 1948. He was a true patriot; it is proper that an aircraft carrier was named for him after his death.

for publication, with the proviso that the article be printed without giving the name of its author. That was the case of the cypher "X" for the article, entitled "The Source of Soviet Conduct," soon to be called the "Containment" article, or even doctrine, published in *Foreign Affairs* in late June 1947 for their July number. Almost immediately after its publication Arthur Krock, a chief columnist for the *New York Times,* revealed that "X" was George Kennan.

The sum of the "X" article was that any further advance of the Soviet Union and communism to the West must be resisted, principally by political means; that to thus contain Soviet ambitions was the present necessity as well as one with reasonable prospects in the long run. The article's reverberations were resounding and instant; its reputation became enormous and enduring, indeed worldwide, indeed to the present day. Ever since, Kennan has been described as the author of the "Containment" doctrine, a designation against which he was to struggle throughout his life: "one of those indestructible myths that are the bane of the historian." Here was another example of unintended consequences — but then a historian cannot eschew a summation of consequences, whether they were intended or not. "Containment" was a success because of its timeliness: for by July 1947 not only the change in the course of the American ship of state but the change of American public opinion about communism and the Soviet Union was just about completed. If Kennan was preaching he was preaching to the converted.* The substance of his "X" article was yet another exposition of what had become obvious. Thus do ideas move in the history of a democracy. Those in charge

---

* Also — that was not the first time that he used the word "contain."

on the highest levels of American government, as well as those in charge of the formulation of American public opinion, found "containment" very much in accord with their views of the world and of Europe: *contain* communism and the Soviet Union; do not let them advance or penetrate anywhere beyond the iron curtain; commit the United States to the defense of western Europe (later: of the "free world"); and thus accept, tacitly or otherwise, the division of Europe. And since that condition — in Europe — continued to exist for more than forty years, until the dissolution of the Soviet empire and of its rule in eastern Europe, "containment" continued (and often still continues) to be regarded as a doctrine, and George Kennan as its wise and prime architect.

This is not how Kennan regarded his article, and the wide reverberation that followed it. He was not pleased with that. (Nor was Marshall, who admonished Kennan for the fact of publication, but he let that go when Kennan told him that he had submitted the article for official permission before sending it to *Foreign Affairs*.) Kennan's reservations about "X" occurred to him instantly, and not only after a year or two in retrospect. He saw two shortcomings of his text. One was the absence of anything about eastern Europe — implying therefore the acceptance of the division of Europe. Another was his insufficient emphasis of the necessary distinction between political and military efforts to contain communism. There was much that was solid and enduring in his text: for example, that the Soviet empire was a weaker construction than it seemed to so many; that the containment of the Soviet Union would, sooner or later, contribute to disunity and weakness of the Communist Party; and, if that would come about one day, "the weakness of Russian society would be revealed in terms beyond description. . . . Soviet Russia might be changed overnight from one of the strongest to one of the weakest and most pitiable of national societies." But overall, "The Sources of Soviet Conduct" emphasized the factor of communism rather than the historical and geographic reality of the Russian empire, even though, as we have seen, Kennan had—and for many years—recognized that communist dogma had no longer much to do with the motives and purposes of Soviet statecraft.

4

The public success of the "X" article left Kennan unimpressed: but he was not indifferent when confronted with contrary opinions of people he respected. Walter Lippmann wrote a series of articles critical of the "X" thesis. Kennan was hurt by what he thought was Lippmann's misreading of some of his arguments: a substantial correspondence ensued and then private discussions between the two men. This was not a matter of great importance: but it contributed to Kennan's sense of loneliness, of his being often misunderstood. That inclination of feeling gnawed at him, affecting his health on occasion, more than overwork that he seldom minded and could cope with amazingly well. After "X" he was very busy, now not so much with speaking invitations but because Marshall gave him assignments added to his tasks with the Policy Planning Staff. A month after the "X" publication Kennan was sent to Paris, to explain the containment policy to some of America's putative western European allies, including the difficult French. His short visit was a success. The French and the British governments were impressed by his exposition—and perhaps by the emerging design of an American foreign policy that seemed to have become committed not only to their material recovery and defense but also to the acceptance of the division of Europe, including that of Germany.

During the next few months the division of Europe began to crystallize. It was now evident that about Germany no agreement was possible with the Russians. In their portion of Berlin, in their zone of East Germany, and in eastern Europe they were dropping their transitional acceptance of the last pro-Russian but still to some extent noncommunist people, replacing them with such that were entirely subordinate to Moscow, not only virtual but actual satellites of the Soviet Union. A remaining, and partial, exception to this was Czechoslovakia.* In a memorandum prepared for Marshall in November 1947 Kennan accurately predicted that this would not last. In Kennan's analysis the brutal clamping down on the last remnants of noncommunist rule in eastern Europe meant that Moscow could no longer permit the existence of a semidemocratic regime and state not entirely closed off from western and central Europe by an iron curtain. Washington and American public opinion saw the communist takeover in Czechoslovakia as a signal of Russia's increasingly aggressive and even warlike intentions. In the spring of 1948 and for some months thereafter there was an anxious fear that "the cold war" (Lippmann's term) might escalate into something like an actual war with Russia. But before that I must turn to the unusual—and, by and large successful—mission of Kennan to Japan.

Kennan's main interests and his main competence involved

---

* And also Finland; but then Finland, exceptional in the Russian sphere of eastern Europe, was unoccupied by a Russian army.

Europe and Russia, not the Far East.* Yet Marshall entrusted him to travel there, for the purpose of attempting some kind of coordination between his strategic policies and those of General MacArthur. The relations between these two generals were not good. Their personalities and their characters were different; so were their priorities during the Second World War. Marshall's priority was Europe, MacArthur's was the Pacific. Added to this were differences between the policies of the State and the War Departments. And even more important than these factors was MacArthur's unique position in Japan: an actual ruler, a virtual viceroy. Kennan was well aware of this. His mission was made easier by the personality and intelligence of the general officer the War Department assigned to accompany him, General Courtlandt Van Rensselaer Schuyler. They landed in Tokyo after a comfortless flight, half-frozen, at the end of February. There MacArthur had neither much respect for nor much interest in discussions with emissaries from Washington. Yet Kennan succeeded — after some difficulties — to get the general to hear him out. On two occasions they met in private; and MacArthur was not indifferent to some of Kennan's ideas. The latter was quite knowledgeable of the former's vanity. Kennan left a magisterial description of their encounter in Tokyo.† By and large

---

*Nor the Middle East. At that very time Kennan opposed the instant American recognition of the state of Israel. In that opposition he was not alone among important officials of the Department of State, including Marshall.

†Another splendid passage from the *Memoirs* demands quotation. After a criticism of American generals abroad who were invested, or who invested themselves, in situations to rule entire countries, Kennan adds that they were not responsible "for the positions in which they found themselves. . . . They deserved the respect which must be paid in general to benevolent

there were no profound differences between them about what had to be done (and not done) in Japan, at least not at that time. Thus Kennan's mission to Tokyo was not unsuccessful.

There was, however, a latent difference separating Kennan's and MacArthur's views about communism and China. That did not come to the fore at that time in Tokyo; but it would affect Kennan's career not much later. General Marshall had returned in late 1946 from his own mission to China, trying to reach some kind of a cease-fire or another arrangement in the then developing civil war between communists and Nationalists. He did not succeed. By and large the communists were winning that civil war. Kennan thought that while that was regrettable, it was not a catastrophe—not for the United States.* As early as in May 1947, in his abovementioned War College speech, he foretold that an eventual victory of the Chinese communists would lead to serious problems for Moscow; that it would compromise and reduce, rather than extend, Russia's influence in the Far East. That was, alas, the very opposite of the slogan the Republican Party employed against President Truman and Marshall and the

---

despotism wherever encountered. I am merely pointing our that these commanders enjoyed something of the same sympathies which I suppose were once addressed to Belisarius by itinerant Byzantines visiting the Italy that rested under his command, enjoying his hospitality, and listening to his complaints about the inept and ignorant interference he had to endure from the imperial court in Constantinople." I fear that such prose (and wisdom) in the words of an American official we shall not see in the next one thousand years.

* He did not think that—whether they pronounced themselves communist or not—what were essentially nationalist uprisings against the vestiges of former colonialism called for American invention—as, for example, in Indochina.

Democrats in 1948–49 and long thereafter: they were accused for having "lost" China to communism (as if China had been there for the United States to lose.) *

When Kennan returned from Tokyo, Czechoslovakia was gone, and there were alarming signs that a crisis over Berlin was opening, possibly even with the prospect of a shooting war. Kennan did not think that would happen. But he was worn, he came down with a gastric ulcer, requiring a hospital stay in April 1948. The crisis of the spring and early summer of that year was on, especially in Europe. There was the tragedy of Czechoslovakia, the beginning of the Russian and East German blockade of Berlin; the pending elections in Italy, where the Communist Party was larger than in any other western European country. The government of the United States chose to intervene in the Italian elections with all kinds of material and political means. Kennan did not think that the Communists would win that election. If they did, he proposed that the United States reoccupy its large wartime air base in the south of Italy. The Christian Democrats won a large victory in those elections. Then something happened in eastern Europe that was not only unforeseen but unnoticed by the State Department until it burst into the open. Tito, the head of Communist Yugoslavia, chose to resist constant and increasing Russian pressures. Moscow then chose to break with him openly and to declare Yugoslavia to be an enemy of the Soviet Union and of its satellites in eastern Europe. Here was an early, and surprising, confirmation of what Kennan had foreseen. The

---

* This kind of propaganda not only led to a mutation in American popular sentiments; it was also one of the reasons why John Foster Dulles would turn against Kennan and remove him from the State Department.

monopoly of Soviet rule over eastern Europe was beginning to crack. His immediate suggestions of how to deal with Tito's Yugoslavia were practical and wise.

Yet around that time his position on the high bridge of the American ship of state had started to weaken. What contributed to that was his nondemocratic (rather than antidemocratic) conviction that his job was to represent and to help chart his country's interests in their relations to other states but not to the politicians of Congress, for many members of which he had little or no respect. His critics would, on occasion, define this as Kennan's "elitism" — wrongly so. He was not a politician, not even remotely so; but neither was he a prototypical diplomat. Throughout his life he did not particularly enjoy either the formalities of embassy dinners or the social chitchat of other diplomatists and their wives. What he enjoyed were conversations about intellectual and historical topics. A self-imposed separateness was an element of his character, and sometimes a symptom of his integrity: but it could impress others as unduly rigid. He had an admirable consideration and respect for his official superiors; but he neither sought nor relished a thorough companionship with people who were, or had become, influential. There was now such a group in Washington, a gathering of such men as Robert Lovett, John McCloy, Clark Clifford, Charles Bohlen (this list is not at all complete), who, together with Acheson (and some of them later under Dulles), were now in charge of assisting with the making of important decisions of American policy about western Europe and Germany. Kennan was not close to them except for Bohlen, his old colleague and friend. At times he took part in their evening and long weekend get-togethers and discussions. They respected and liked him, but they also knew that he was something of an outsider. They and their wives made a few weekend visits to the Kennan farm in southern Pennsylvania; they found their hosts' hospitality easy and thoughtful, though the rather spartan conditions, including his habit of having his guests help with gardening or housework, perhaps less so. But of course much more important than that was one latent disagreement — or, rather, a difference of emphasis — between them and Kennan. They were, by and large, satisfied with and committed to "containing" Russia and communists, to maintain and secure the division of Europe (and of Germany). Kennan was not.

Here I must pause for a moment in order to say something about the origins of the Cold War. The accepted view was then, and is even now, largely correct. The United States had to react against the aggressive behavior of the Soviet Union. Some, mostly second- and third-rate, historians and others committed to special pleading and to selective indignation argued, especially in the 1960s, that this American reaction was excessive and premature. Their arguments or reconstructions or interpretations were insubstantial. The very opposite of what they wrote was true. The American reaction in 1946–47 was not premature but overdue; not too early but (as Kennan saw it) almost too late. Still — there is a latent, and important, difference among those, too, who thought and think that the American response in 1947 was largely right. The difference is between those who thought that the main threat to western Europe and to the United States was communism; and those, like Kennan, who thought that the main issue was not communism but Russia, not ideological but historical and territorial. It may even be argued that the Cold War, as it developed, was the outcome of a reciprocal misunderstanding. By 1947 Americans, and their government, believed that the Soviet Union, having won eastern Europe, was now ready to expand further into western Europe — which was not really the case. By 1947 Stalin began to fear that the United States was ready to challenge his rule over eastern Europe — which, too, was not the case. Kennan thought that Stalin was neither ready nor willing (and surely not militarily) to expand further in Europe, not even in Germany.* In this Kennan was, more than probably, right.

But now we must come to an, often obscured, subchapter of his career: something that went unmentioned in his *Memoirs,* and that he would later privately regret. This was his propagation, mostly in 1948, to stir up some trouble in eastern Europe, by so-called "covert" operations there.

Some of this was due to his unwillingness to accept an enduring division of Europe and of Germany. But there was another element in his mind too. This was the long overdue need to establish instruments assisting America's foreign relations. Now that the necessary change in the course of the American ship of state had been set, some changes had to be made in the instrumentation of its progress. There is (and there will remain) little documentary evidence about the establishment and the actual operations of "covert" or "clandestine" or "secret" institutions. Such is the nature of governments, democratic or not; and Kennan himself was knowledgeable enough to leave few written records about these matters, including his private papers. But there

---

* He thought, and mentioned this decades later, that Stalin did not want an all-Communist Germany: for, if that would happen, Moscow would soon lose its predominance in international Communism, perhaps even including Russia's recently acquired domains: the center might move from Moscow to Berlin.

is enough documentary residue to sketch or even to sum up these matters, no matter how briefly. To begin with: Kennan was instrumental in proposing the need for an American Central Intelligence Agency in 1948. He had a fair amount of experience in dealing with intelligence matters in the past (perhaps especially in Lisbon in 1943). More important: he was, ever so often, distressed and irritated by the conflicting, uncoordinated, amateurish, sometimes overeager activities of various American intelligence agencies, especially of those of the Office of Strategic Services during the war and of the different Defense intelligence agencies thereafer. It was therefore that he proposed the establishment of a Central (and civilian-ruled) Intelligence Agency — many of whose activities and whose very existence he later came to regret, and ruefully indeed: "The greatest mistake I ever made."* In April and May 1948 he proposed "a 'directorate' for overt and covert political warfare" — one kept out of the military agencies and subordinated to the Department of State. Upon his recommendation an Office of Special Projects was instituted there, under his leadership, and approved by the president.

Soon it appeared that this limitation, too, was illusory. The Office of Special Projects would not last long. He found it impossible to restrict this office and its operations to the State Department. Still — in 1948 and early 1949 Kennan was able to arrange very secret matters that he deemed important for the national interest of the United States. Among other things these included the clandestine importation of certain Germans, some

---

* Kennan to Wilson D. Miscamble, *George F. Kennan and the Making of American Foreign Policy, 1947–1950*, Princeton, 1992, p. 109: a superb study of Kennan during those years; among many others perhaps the best.

of whom Kennan had known during the war in Berlin and Moscow, and whose knowledge of Russian matters could be very useful.* Meanwhile, President Truman accepted the recommendations of the Office of Special Projects, including its proposition for "covert" operations beyond the iron curtain. National Security Council directive no. 10/2 was signed by the president in November. Before that, in August, Kennan drafted a memorandum entitled "U.S. Objectives Towards Russia." In this, among other matters, he wrote that while the Soviet Union would not take military action to expand westward beyond the iron curtain, at the same time the Soviet Union was most vulnerable within its recently acquired large domain of satellite states in eastern Europe. He insisted that promoting the eventual dissolution of the Soviet domain in eastern Europe must not involve an American policy aiming at the dissolution of the Soviet Union proper (even as he suggested that the Soviet regime itself might have to face the danger of its own crisis in ten or fifteen years).

All of this may prove that in 1948 Kennan was at his peak as a Cold War Warrior. Yet, against all evidences on the surface, his influence was already lessening in Washington; and — this is important — his views of the Cold War and of the world were drifting away, more and more, from the main course preferred by others.

---

*Many of these former German officials were honest and unexceptionable. The most stunning (and shocking) of these German imports was no less a Nazi personage than General Heinrich Müller, head of the Gestapo, who after the war survived in Switzerland. (About him see my article, "The Churchill-Roosevelt Forgeries," in *American Heritage,* November–December 2002, p. 66.) It seems — we cannot be certain — that Müller's importation into the United States was arranged by Allen Dulles, in 1948. Whether Kennan knew about the Müller case I cannot tell.

Less than a year after his "Containment" article, where he left the matter of eastern Europe unmentioned, he was now thinking about the potential importance of eastern Europe, while others, in general, were ignoring it. He wished to correct (correct, rather than terminate) the division of Europe.* In 1948 he regarded the Yugoslav-Soviet conflict as very significant; he was also fascinated by what was happening to Finland, a country within the Russian sphere of interest, yet one on whose Communization Stalin chose not to insist.† This idea, and prospect, of the eventual "Finlandization" of at least some of eastern Europe was a consistent element in Kennan's views not only in 1948 but during four decades thereafter, throughout the Cold War — no matter whether he was seen by some of his critics as a prime Cold Warrior or as an Appeaser. It was part and parcel of his desideratum not to accept the division of Europe as permanent — and to propose reciprocal Russian and American withdrawals from the center of the continent.

That was not the main American policy in 1948–49 and not for more than forty years. What the ruling powers in Washington accepted were marginal policies affecting eastern Europe, with their purpose of causing troubles for the Soviet Union. The establishment of the Central Intelligence Agency, of a few "covert" operations in eastern Europe, of something called Psychological

---

* "He sought to preserve the possibility of his larger objective — the retraction of Soviet power from Eastern Europe." Miscamble, *Kennan,* p. 161, citing PPS records.

† For two reasons: one was Stalin's respect for the Finnish capacity to resist and fight; the other (even more significant in Kennan's eyes) was Stalin's choice to leave Finland relatively free, as long as its neighbor Sweden would not abandon its neutrality by joining an American alliance system.

Warfare, of the Free Europe Committee, of powerful radio stations such as Radio Free Europe and Radio Liberty — all of these took place in late 1948 and 1949. All of these endeavors Kennan supported at that time.* Yet his influence, and the importance of his office, were lessening. In more than one instance men such as Robert Lovett told Kennan that *the* most important matter of this or that policy was to assure its support in Congress. Then, at the very end of 1948, General Marshall's tenure as secretary of state ended. He was succeeded by Dean Acheson, whose interest in the policy Planning Staff (and in the Office of Special Projects) was limited from the beginning and led to the virtual abolition of the latter one year later.

5

Readers, at this point, must not have the impression that from now on, from late 1948 and thereafter, the decline of Kennan's role and influence in Washington was uninterrupted. His future

---

*One exception to the general policy of the American (and British) governments in eastern Europe was the case of Albania. There were no Russian troops in that small and misery-laden country. Alone among the eastern European Communist states Albania had not been given a military alliance with Moscow, and now in 1948 it was separated from the Soviet sphere by Tito's Yugoslavia. Therefore it was natural and reasonable (especially in the eyes of the British) to intervene — of course secretly — in Albania, and attempt an eventual overthrow of the Communist regime there, mostly by infiltrating anticommunist Albanian groups by sea and, on occasion, by air. I do not know how much of Kennan's Special Projects group was involved in these activities; but I am inclined to think that he approved that plan. However: these plans collapsed mostly because a British secret planner involved in them (Kim Philby) was a Soviet spy. Also, most of this happened in late 1949, when Kennan's influence was already in decline.

biographers will have a difficult task separating the many entangling threads of his official life during the two years that followed. One difficulty is the accumulation of the crises of the Cold War in 1948 and 1949 that we may, in retrospect, see as its peak and most dangerous period: to wit, the Berlin blockade, the formation of NATO, the first Russian atomic bomb — at a time when Kennan still remained an important adviser to the government. And, in addition to the monstrous mass of documents spewed out by the ever growing bureaucracies in Washington, there are hundreds if not thousands of pages of Kennan's private diaries and papers, many of which are telling as well as illuminating: an embarrassment of riches for any biographer, as well as for the writer of this book attempting not much more than a narrative study of George Kennan's character. But disentangling this entangled skein of events he, too, must attempt.

Kennan was still in the Far East and then in the hospital in March and April 1948, when the end of Czechoslovakia, the beginning of the blockade of West Berlin, and the potentiality of sudden war gripped Washington. He did not believe that Stalin was planning anything like a war; he also saw and said that the Soviet aim to eliminate the American-Western presence in Berlin, even though shameless and brutal, was from Stalin's point of view defensive. President Truman's resolution and the developing success of the airlift to Berlin eased the tension at that critical point, and less than a year later the Russians abandoned the blockade. But Berlin was but part of the larger question of Germany in which Kennan and his Policy Planning Staff were much involved through that year. His emphatic interest and knowledge of Germany and of things German should have led to accepting him as much as a German as a Russian expert: but that was not really what happened. In 1948 and 1949 he was heard rather than listened to; others, not he, were in charge of America's German policy. About one matter he was largely in agreement with what was happening in 1948: the merging of the three western zones of occupation, the establishment of something like a West German state, with its own currency and constitution, a western Germany firmly bound to the rest of western Europe. But at the same time he argued against accepting an enduring division of Germany. When in the fall of 1948 preparations were made for yet another foreign ministers meeting with the Russians, who now seemed to take the division of Germany and of Berlin for granted (for Stalin, too, half of Germany was better than none), Marshall still asked Kennan and his staff to prepare a memorandum about Germany. Kennan was the author of that, named Plan A. It called for the proposition of a united, demilitarized, and "neutral" all-German government, together with a reciprocal withdrawal of Russian and American and Western forces from the center to the peripheries of a new German state. He thought it worthwhile to propose such a plan to the Russians and then see their response. Yet it was not the Russians but the powers in Washington who thought it best not to propose Kennan's plan.

He knew that. He knew that his influence had become weaker. (There were even signs that some of his Planning Staff were not in accord with him.) However, he was not cast aside; he was still respected and, on occasion, listened to. We have seen that Dean Acheson, the new secretary of state, cared less for the Policy Planning Staff than had General Marshall. But Acheson still told Kennan to continue with his work, and also gave Kennan opportunities to travel. In March and April 1949 Kennan flew to

Germany. He spent considerable time there, staying in Berlin, Frankfurt, Hamburg, Bremen — all cities that he knew so well before 1941. The long passages of his diaries, their descriptions and observations and sentiments, are masterpieces of his writing. (Was this why, nearly two decades later, he found it proper to reproduce some of them at length in his *Memoirs*?) They were not always realistic. His descriptions were melancholy and pessimistic, his observations were sharp and critical — he found the high living and the insensitivity of the American occupation personnel and of their dependents distasteful, rightly so; but he was wrong not to see that by 1949 the sudden and amazing revitalization of material life in western Germany, the so-called *Wirtschaftswunder,* the "economic miracle," was already running in full course.

Years later he saw (and wrote) that his dark pessimism about Germany in 1949 was not warranted. But he remained consistent in his belief that the long-range acceptance of the division of Europe and of Germany was wrong. Looking at the political geography of Europe he saw that some states in or near the center of the continent did not (or at least did not entirely) belong to either Russia or to the American-dominated military bloc: such as Sweden, Switzerland, Austria, Yugoslavia, perhaps even Finland. He hoped — but more and more hoping against hope — that this might be extended to Germany too. That was not about to happen. Instead, in 1949, NATO, the North Atlantic Treaty Organization, was born. That was a milestone, a great step in the history of the United States: for the first time its government was willing to agree to a permanent stationing of American forces in the Old World even in — relative — peacetime. To that move Kennan was not opposed; but to its extensions and instrumentation very much so. We have seen that his interpretation for "containing" Russia and communism was principally not military but political, or military only where and when obviously necessary. He favored a close American alliance with Canada and Britain, together with a political and military alliance of a revived western Europe. He thought that the inclusion, by Acheson and others, of states such as Greece and Turkey into a "North Atlantic" alliance was a mockery.

But by the time NATO was formed his influence was more and more limited. After September 1949 the Policy Planning Staff no longer had direct access to the secretary of state. There were, more than often tacit and latent, differences between Kennan and other members of the Planning Staff. He arrived at the conclusion that the work of policy planning had become useless. Still, Acheson insisted and convinced Kennan to stay in government service "on absence without pay."*

* In December 1949 Acheson made a public statement about Kennan's departure "that filled me with despair. He is one of the most distinguished, if not the most distinguished Foreign Service Officer. I have rarely met a man the depth of whose thought, the sweetness of whose nature combined to bring about a real understanding of the underlying problems of modern life. But after I thought about the questions of his taking a sabbatical leave, it seemed it was the right and good thing to do." Webb papers, in the Harry S. Truman Library, box 20, cited in Miscamble, *Kennan,* p. 296.

# Washington to Princeton

I

Nearly five years in his official career would still follow. Whether we call them "Ups and Downs" or "Limbo" "or "Purgatory" does not matter. He called them "Transition." For him the importance of this gradual, and interrupted, transition from what I called "officer on the high bridge of the ship of state" to a different kind of life may appear from the many pages he devoted to them in his *Memoirs:* 132 pages (out of 500) in the first, 189 (out of 324) in the second, thus more than one-third in an autobiography encompassing about forty years. This reflects how enduring and lasting his devotion to the cause of his country's relations to the world was, and remained — and also how the transition of his life from statesman to scholar, from diplomatist to historian, was never complete. But transition it was — involving, among other important matters, giving up their house in Washington and then moving to Princeton in August 1950.

Yet he remained on the rolls as a Foreign Service officer until June 1953.

These were difficult years for him and for his family. But they had had plenty of experiences with difficult years before. Again the quiet and steady reasonableness of his wife was invaluable for him, perhaps especially in his dark and untempered moments.

2

When in September 1949 the news of the first Soviet atomic bomb came to a rattled Washington, Kennan was no longer the active head of the Policy Planning Staff. He wrote — as so often — an unsolicited memorandum about that event. He set forth, for the first time, the principle which he would state a decade and then another decade later: that the United States should commit itself never to make "first use" of its own atomic weapons. He also questioned the necessity of producing a new and more powerful variant, the so-called hydrogen bomb, the construction of which President Truman approved at the very time when Kennan hoped that his memorandum would circulate. (He had no evidence whether either the secretary of state or other high officials read it.) In any event he, at that time, did not attribute exceptional importance to the Russians' possession of an atomic bomb. That was in accord with his general belief that armaments alone do not make history: it is history — or, within it, the governments of competing states — that make armaments, the use of which depends on the relations of states. An obvious truth — to which we may add George Kennan's skepticism not only of the questionable benefits but of the questionable effectiveness of technology and of its innovations.

In February 1950 he left for an unusual tour of Central and South America. It seems that this was his own plan, but the State Department underwrote it materially and politically, with the unfortunate result that much publicity about it was generated in some South American cities upon Kennan's arrival, leading to scattered demonstrations against him. That was of course unpleasant: but then his entire journey through the southern half of the Americas was overcast by the saturnine side of his temperament. His descriptions and his conclusions of Mexico, Venezuela, Brazil, Peru were dark and replete with coruscating illuminations by his pen of what he saw and heard: scenes of gimcrack façades and waste, of masses of glitter and dust, of violent noises and morbid silences, of pompous phrases empty of sincerity, honesty, meaning. His sardonic summaries of what he saw as a fatally flawed civilization disconcerted even some of his remaining associates on the planning staff.*

He was still away in South America when *Reader's Digest* published an article of his in March 1950 which is remarkable in retrospect. I do not know who and what originated this short article in a popular magazine and who gave it the title "Is War with Russia Inevitable?" What is telling is Kennan's response to that crude rhetorical question: No.† Very telling, too, is what he said at his commencement address at Dartmouth College on 11 June: "In war, as in no other human undertaking, the modern

---

* Fifteen years later he felt compelled to revise his funereal assessments. He wrote that, perhaps, South America might be one of the last repositories of a fragmented and rapidly declining "Western" civilization.

† Among other matters he stated that in eastern Europe the Soviet Union "bit off more than it could comfortably chew" and that the Soviet military threat, including their atomic bomb, must not be exaggerated.

form of popular nationalism rises up to assert itself as the dominant political force in our times."*

A fortnight later, on Sunday, 25 June 1950, the news of the North Korean invasion of South Korea burst on an unsuspecting, nay, somnolent Washington. Kennan was at his farm in Pennsylvania. He knew nothing until he and his wife were driving back to their Washington apartment late in the afternoon and then saw the headlines. He repaired to the State Department immediately. Acheson went off to the airport to meet the president, who was flying in from Missouri. Acheson's secretary told Kennan and a few others that Acheson wished them to come to Blair House for dinner with the president. At the last minute, immediately before they were to leave, Acheson's secretary told Kennan that he was not on the list of those expected thither. This, it seems, was not the result of some conscious decision or intrigue but a bureaucratic mishap. Aware that Kennan's departure from the government was presently due, Acheson asked him to postpone that step, in order to be available to the government during the fast-developing Korean crisis.

Kennan's recommendations and contributions during the Korean War are in the public domain, within the enormous mass of papers documenting especially the critical months as the war proceeded during the second half of 1950. There were three developments worth mentioning here. The first comprised his

---

* Two other remarkable sentences: "A knowledge of human history should have warned us, perhaps, against the assumption that material things and gadgets might have more than a limited bearing on human happiness." Also: unless men adopt the "selflessness and compassion toward their fellow men, as Christ once [did], our civilization may be facing an early and dreadful end."

recommendations that may be summed up briefly. He agreed with the others that a swift and definite American military response to the North Korean aggression must be made. He also (unlike MacArthur) insisted that the military aim should be the restoration of the former state of things, that the North Koreans, once successfully repelled, should not be pursued beyond the division line of the 38th parallel. The second matter was that he, unlike some others, saw that the aims and the policies of the Russian and of the Chinese Communists (the latter had only recently become the masters of mainland China) were not the same. The Chinese wanted now to be admitted to the United Nations, including its Security Council. Kennan thought that there was no great danger in that. It did not mean an official American diplomatic recognition of Communist China; it opened at least one chance toward negotiations to settle the Korean War; and it suggested the possibility of differences between the Soviet Union and Communist China in the Far East. Again his recommendations were heard but not followed. And here we come to a third event or development, which was John Foster Dulles's hostility to George Kennan.

Dulles was brought into the counsels of American foreign policy by Harry Truman, in the interests of "bipartisanship," about two years before. This is not the place to describe or analyze this man's character; we should be interested in him only inasmuch as he affected George Kennan's career and life. In that respect hostility may not be too strong a word. Whether its main root was ideological or personal I cannot tell: probably both; and for our purposes this does not matter. During the discussions about Korea, Dulles found it proper, at least on one occasion, to shout at Kennan. A few days later Kennan was informed of what

Dulles had told a journalist: "that while he used to think highly of George Kennan he had now concluded that the latter was a very dangerous man; that he was advocating the admission of the Chinese Communists to the United Nations and a cessation of U.S. military action at the 38th parallel."

Less than a month later Kennan wrote a most pessimistic passage in his diary, with which, fifteen or sixteen years later, he chose to conclude the first volume of his *Memoirs*. The gist of it was that the confusion of minds in Washington was hopeless, such that no one, including the president, really understood what was going on. That was one of Kennan's exaggerations, issuing from his moods. In the short run he may have been right. MacArthur sent American divisions into North Korea, beyond the 38th parallel; the Russians did little; however, the Chinese did; they entered the war, forcing these American divisions to retreat southward in bitter winter weather. But it was now Acheson who suddenly sought, and received, support from Kennan. The sequence of what now happened is worth reconstructing. On 1 December, in retirement at his farm, Kennan received an unexpected international telephone call from Bohlen in Paris. His old friend urged Kennan to make Washington know that he was available, because of his understanding of the Soviet Union, whose presence in the Far East was now a very important factor. Next day Kennan told the Department of State that he would come if and when needed. He arrived at the State Department early on the morning of 3 December, a Sunday. That was, for Washington, the darkest day of the entire Korean War. Kennan found the officials at the department despondent, even panicky. To most of them it seemed that an entire American withdrawal from all of Korea was becoming inevitable; they also thought that unavoidably, too, there was now need for an urgent American approach to Russia, in search of its eventual help in getting an armistice. Kennan rejected both of these arguments. To approach the Russians now would be nothing but a signal of weakness.* It was evening when Kennan came into Acheson's room. He was stunned to see the secretary tired and worn. Suddenly he got up and asked Kennan to come home with him for dinner and stay the night in their house if must. There they talked (and drank) at length. During that most somber of nights George Kennan, ever so often suffused with a sense of gloom, strengthened and helped Acheson's resolution. Then, true to his habits and himself, he rose at dawn and wrote a longhand letter to Acheson.† Acheson found it on his desk first thing in the morning. He was so moved by it that he read it aloud to his staff before everything else.

He would not let George Kennan depart from his service to his country. John Foster Dulles did. But before that, two and a half more years were to pass.

3

Exactly six months later it became Kennan's task to attempt nothing less than to settle the Korean War, ending it through an armistice. It is curious that he devoted in his *Memoirs* little space and not much emphasis to this most important effort, which is described in greater detail in the memoir written by Acheson, and

---

* This writer finds it worthwhile to note that one of Kennan's opponents in these discussions was Dean Rusk, then a partisan of withdrawal; many years later — again unlike Kennan — a "hawk" about Russia and communism.
† This is reproduced in the Appendix, pages 191–92.

a more or less precise reconstruction of which remains a subject for future research. The essential circumstance was that MacArthur's trumpeting of Unconditional Surrender had obviously failed (notwithstanding the enormous popular clamor in his favor after President Truman removed him), while Kennan's advocacy for considering "limited wars" (a conviction that long preceded the Korean crisis) had become a reality in that unhappy land. Exactly a month after Truman fired MacArthur, Stewart Alsop (a close friend of Acheson's who also knew Kennan) wrote an article in the *New York Herald Tribune* comparing Kennan's view to MacArthur's, adding that Kennan "was reported to believe" that there ought to be at least one diplomatic effort to sound out the Russians whether "at least some temporary settlement" could be made. A few days later Acheson sent a message to Kennan to come to Washington. Kennan should get in touch with Jacob Malik, the Russian representative at the United Nations. They could speak confidentially between themselves, among other circumstances because of Kennan's knowledge of Russian. A fortnight later Kennan and Malik had two such secret meetings, without an interpreter. Another fortnight later Malik, somewhat obliquely, announced that the Soviet government was in favor of an armistice in Korea. By that time fighting there had settled down; the two sides had begun to dig themselves in approximately along the 38th parallel (a border that has remained during fifty-five years, to this day). More than a year later General Eisenhower, candidate for the presidency, declared, "I shall go to Korea" to secure peace. In reality, by June 1951 the Korean War was over.

At least some of that was due to George Kennan. We have seen before that he was not an expert on the Far East. But there was at least something like a parallel in his analyses (there were not a few, written as early as 1948) of the situation in the Far East and in that of central Europe. In both cases and in both of these parts of the world he believed that the Russians had no inclination to expand further; and that subsequently there were reasons to explore reciprocal military withdrawals: leading, in Europe, to a demilitarized and neutral Germany and Austria, and in the Far East to a demilitarized and neutral Japan and Korea. Whether such plans would have succeeded, or even whether they would have been propitious and advantageous for the United States at that time, we cannot tell. They did not happen. What happened was a permanent American military alliance with Japan, and then a permanent American military alliance with West Germany — both, in essence, lasting till this day, even beyond the end of the Cold War and the collapse of the Soviet sphere of interest. But there was another, and related, conviction in Kennan's mind that remains timely to this day. Save for the, to him, unavoidable American response to the North Korean aggression in 1950, he warned against any and every kind of American military intervention on the mainland of Asia. He warned too, as early as in 1948 and in many of his writings thereafter, against the, unfortunately traditional, American inclinations toward and expectations from China. His tireless reading of historic Chinese and Korean relations with Russia only confirmed his view. He foresaw conflicts between Moscow and Peking long before these became apparent. I even make bold to say that when it came to conflicts between Russians and Chinese, Kennan would incline to favor the former — the very opposite of the policies that such different presidents as Nixon and Carter and Reagan and Clinton and now, more than a half-century later, Bush had chosen to take.

4

In the spring of 1952 Kennan was made American ambassador to Moscow. This was the peak point of his official career. Six years before that he was a forlorn man in Moscow, beset with despair about his government's views of Russia. Few, himself included, would have believed that one day he would be the principal envoy of the United States to the second greatest power in the world. But this has now happened. He was chosen by the secretary of state and by President Truman himself, who told this to Kennan in so many words. He was confirmed by the Foreign Relations Committees of the Senate and the House, composed mostly of Republicans, unanimously.

Yet he was, to say the least, of two minds about this. He said to Acheson that they should consider choosing someone else, but he was told that the president wanted him. Kennan thought that it was his duty to accept this assignment, for which he was especially qualified because of his knowledge and experience. Beyond and beneath that obvious condition doubts and premonitions existed in his mind. His views of Russia were not quite in accord with Acheson's and not with the course taken by the government in general. He took some satisfaction from his farewell call on the president, who said that he did not believe that the Soviet leaders wanted war. But that was all. He was more than saddened, he was depressed by the condition that he had no instructions — not from the president, not from Acheson, not from anyone else in Washington — about what was to be expected from him in Moscow, what the principal aims of the government in its relations to Moscow should now be. Then he asked for another, last meeting with Acheson and the latter's top advisers. They listened to him but paid not much attention to his ideas and questions. He returned from Washington to Princeton with a heavy heart.

In retrospect we may be permitted to suggest that while his appointment to Moscow was proof of the respect he had earned and still had in Washington, the then present view, including that of the secretary of state, was that the role of America's ambassador to Moscow was now not very important. His presence there was desirable; his opinions and reports from there might be of *some* interest; but his role in influencing America's relationship with the Soviet Union for the present was minimal; he would continue to represent, rather than to advise. Kennan sensed this from the beginning. Then, at the very time of his appointment procedures, a new development occurred. In March 1952 Stalin suddenly made a new proposal about Germany. It called for the establishment of a united and democratic and demilitarized neutral Germany, including even the prospect of all-German elections, while requiring the withdrawal of military occupation forces from that country, both from West and East. Kennan thought that, even if unclear and hidden with potential troubles and dangers, this was worth considering — or, at least, thinking about. Washington did not. (Neither did the British or French or the West German governments.) Washington did not wish to explore, or even discuss, any potential agreement with Moscow regarding Germany. He hoped, against hope, that he would get some kind of reaction from his government to the Stalin Note. There was to be none.

He arrived in Moscow in early May, alone. His youngest child (Wendy) was about to be born; his wife* and their two-year-old

---

* It is noteworthy that she bore this child in her mid-forties.

son would follow later. His presence in Moscow came at what was to be the lowest point in American-Soviet relations. There is no need to describe the atmosphere in Moscow, which was much worse than even in 1946. Stalin had opted for a Russia that was isolationist, which meant, among other things, the isolation (even more than segregation) of foreign diplomats from contacts with almost any Russian; this included, too, close and constant secret police accompaniment and supervision. Because of his great interest in Russia, because of his affection for its people, Kennan was even more pained by these conditions than were other diplomatists posted in Moscow. Yet his mind — and pen — were as active as ever. In one of his letters he described, at length, what he saw one weekend, spent at a suburban dacha outside of Moscow, the teeming everyday life of Russian people in their cabins and market gardens, their energetic handiwork in their small worlds without machines, unmoved and untouched by the impositions and the propaganda of their regime. At the same time the violence and the rabid lies of their government directed at America and Americans were such that, at least on one occasion, he came close to suggesting that while an American diplomatic representation should remain, there might be no need for an American ambassador in Moscow. He was unhappy with some of the activities of his government too. He tried — on occasion, more or less successfully — to curb such American military undertakings that, close to the Soviet Union's frontiers, would unnecessarily arouse Russian suspicions and countermeasures. In early September he sat down at his desk and — again — wrote a long paper for Washington, entitled "The Soviet Union and the Atlantic Pact." In this he warned against excessive militarization on the part of the West, because of the condition that the Soviet Union did not want another war and did not plan to extend further militarily. This dispatch was comparable to the Long Telegram of 1946 but only to some extent; it went largely unnoticed by Washington. But what vexed Kennan above all were his experiences of his sequestered life in Moscow. The result was his — unexpected — explosion, and the subsequent end of his ambassadorial career.

The explosion consisted of a few words. He was requested to fly to London, where a conference of American ambassadors in Europe was to meet. On his way to London his plane stopped in Berlin. At the airport a reporter — among others — approached him with a rather senseless question. Did the embassy have many social contacts with Russians in Moscow? Kennan was angry and impatient. He said that his isolation enforced in Moscow was comparable to how he was interned in Nazi Germany in 1941–42 after the declaration of war.

He went on to London. There he found that the other American ambassadors and the military officers present at that meeting were committed to a policy to perpetuate the division of Germany and of Europe, a policy quite in accord with the views of John Foster Dulles. (Note that this London meeting took place still before the 1952 presidential election and that this was the consensus of ambassadors who had been appointed by Truman.) Kennan was in agony. He seriously thought that he ought to give up his ambassadorship in Moscow. There was no need for that. He was still in London when he was furiously attacked by the Soviet press for what he had said at the airport in Berlin. A few days later the Soviet government officially informed the American embassy that Kennan was now *persona non grata:* he must be immediately recalled from his post as ambassador; and he would not be permitted to return to Moscow to gather his family and pack up.*

He thought that he had been a failure. He had and he hadn't. There are ample reasons to think that Stalin, personally, wanted him out of Moscow, where about Russia and Russians Kennan knew and understood too much. His outburst at the Berlin airport, on the other hand, was intemperate and undiplomatic. He received not much sympathy when he with his family returned to the United States a month later. The next long (and bitter) winter months he spent at the farm. Neither the new president, Eisenhower, nor his new secretary of state, Dulles, made any attempt to contact him. He was still a Foreign Service official on duty but without any assignment. He waited and waited. (Impatience was one recurrent feature of his mind, so often with the result of his urge to write.) In January he accepted an invitation to speak at the convention of the Pennsylvania Bar Association in Scranton. He wrote his speech carefully and had its text properly cleared by the State Department. There were (and there remain) two noteworthy elements in his address. One was his warning that, despotic and alien and even hostile as other governments in the world may be, it must not be the policy of the United States to attempt to overthrow them. Totalitarian governments will, sooner or later, prove to be self-destructive. But —

---

*The heroine in these days was Annelise, with only two days to pack up, which she did "with a dignity and composure that was the admiration of everyone in the embassy and the diplomatic colony."

more significantly — he ended this speech by invoking the perennially profound and wise words of John Quincy Adams in 1823: "We are friends of liberty all over the world; but we do not go abroad in search of monsters to destroy." Future biographers should note that this was the first occasion when Kennan cited these words, mined from the accumulated wealth of his historical knowledge. It may be his gift that this famous old phrase is better known now, more than sixty years later, as apposite for the foreign policy of the United States. He would cite it again and again, often in the 1990s, during the last decade of his life.

That Kennan in this speech, contrary to Dulles, refused to advocate active American intervention in eastern Europe and Russia was noticed and commented upon by two leading newspapers. He now thought it best to go to Washington and tell Dulles, among other things, that the entire text had been cleared by the department; also that he was available for further service. Dulles did not respond. A few weeks later an article in the *New York Times* reported that Kennan would be retired from the Foreign Service. Dulles now called Kennan to come to Washington. He told him that he had "no niche" for him. At a second (their last) meeting in April he suggested to Kennan that he be appointed to an important position with the Central Intelligence Agency. Kennan said that he did not want that. He still hoped that, proper to his talents and his experience, he should have a position in the Foreign Service. But the official termination of his service would come three months later. Before that time he still kept going to Washington. He occupied a desk somewhere on the lower levels of the State Department building, where he worked and read and wrote. There, too, he was now alone. He found few old friends or acquaintances in the department, where Dulles was installing a new crew.

There was one last, and unexpected, episode within that last chapter of George Kennan's government service. President Eisenhower's respect for Kennan was — at least somewhat — higher than that of his secretary of state; but Eisenhower, too, ignored Kennan after his return from Russia, and did nothing to stay Dulles's decision to force Kennan's retirement. However, Eisenhower's then confidant, C. D. Jackson, a powerful panjandrum of Time-Life, an interloper in statecraft and an eager beaver, admired Kennan, contacted him, and spoke to him about his own ideas of "psychological warfare." There is some evidence that Kennan's response to Jackson's ideas was not dismissive and was perhaps even positive. This happened in March — which suggests that even at that time Kennan was still willing and wishing to be consulted by the government. Nothing came out of this. But Jackson may have had something to do with what happened a month or two later, only a few weeks before the terminal date of Kennan's retirement. Eisenhower decided to convoke a highly secret group of men to advise him about his policies regarding the Soviet Union. This "Solarium" conference was named after a room in the White House, though most of the meetings took place in the National War College. One of the "research teams" was headed by Kennan. His summary proposals, mostly involving Germany, were not at all in accord with the policies of Dulles, who, on the last day, sat — together with the entire Eisenhower cabinet — in a large room beneath the main floor of the White House, forced to listen to Kennan (to whose paper the president at least seemed to hear, but whose consequences were nil). That day was the end of the Transition (or Limbo, or Purgatory) years, rather than the day in June when Kennan packed up his remaining papers and said good-bye to the Department of State, where he found no one to say farewell to, except for a kindly lady receptionist whom he had known for years. About that day he left us a beautiful and melancholy two pages in his *Memoirs*.

Alone, he drove north to his farm, where on that warm summer afternoon he was alone too, since his family were out for a few hours. But what was now complete was his final move from Washington not to the farm but to Princeton. We saw that he came to Princeton first in September 1950; but we saw that his and his family's settling there was interrupted by his duties to his government, and often. We shall turn to the conditions and to the prospect of his employment at the Institute for Advanced Studies in Princeton momentarily. Before that something must be said about his Princeton house. "Everything suffers from translation," Trollope once wrote, "except for a bishop" — to which I shall add: except for Kennan. At first they were lodged in one of the houses provided by the Institute. Then he and Anne-lise bought a house on Hodge Street, a quiet region of the town, with little traffic, a wide street with large trees. Years before they had much work to do with rebuilding the old farmhouse and its outbuildings; there was work to be done on the house in Princeton too. It had been built a good forty or fifty years before. It was, and became, admirably fitted not only to their needs but to their personalities: a house once a modest American upper-middle-class dwelling but also with something of a northern European look, with an atmosphere of bourgeois comfort, it was to be their home and refuge for more than a half-century, longer even than his attachment to his farm.

There, in that harbor, he dropped his anchor. But this metaphor does not really fit. This house, this harbor in Princeton was not the end but the beginning of other journeys and the beginning of the second half—in more than one way, the larger half—of his life.

# FIVE

# A Conscience of a Nation

I

The English writer Jean Rhys once wrote that a novel has to have a plot but that life doesn't have any. This is largely true, for all kinds of reasons: one of them being that in a novel the writer intends every event or act or word to have eventual consequences, whereas in a man's life so many consequences are unknown and unexpected and unintended. Yet there are times when certain consequences are decisive enough so that, in retrospect, they give a definite form to the history of a life, as if that had a "plot." That was the case of George Kennan. God gave him a long life, longer than an entire century. His life divides, chronologically but also logically, into two, almost equal, halves: the first fifty years of the student and diplomatist and high government official; the second of the scholar and the historian, lasting more than fifty years, and in a place and situation that suited him better and allowed him more freedom than the first. Toward the end of the first fifty years of his life he became — and began to be recognized as — a helmsman of the American ship of state. During the second half he became — and was recognized by a few — a national treasure.

The two parts cannot, of course, be entirely separated. Chronologically and geographically yes; otherwise no. What binds Acts One and Two together was his impulse to write, his concern with the state and the prospect of his nation. The subjects of his writing varied, but the emphasis of his concerns only seldom. The conditions and the circumstances of his life in Princeton were very different from those before; but the impulses and directions of his mind changed not; they remained, by and large, the same till the end.

A short description of the conditions and circumstances of his life at Princeton cannot now be avoided. In some ways they were ideal. His position in the Institute for Advanced Study was of nearly limitless freedom: he could do what he wanted to do (besides, his financial situation, too, was secure). His portrait of the Institute and of himself in the first chapter of the second volume of his *Memoirs* is an unusual compound of a place that was perfect together with what he remembered as shortcomings of his own mind. It was Robert Oppenheimer who invited and arranged Kennan's coming to the Institute in 1950. Kennan's portrait of Oppenheimer is suffused with gratitude and with his enduring appreciation of Oppenheimer. He has other descriptions, too, of scholars who were now his colleagues at the Institute and whom he esteemed highly. He had, I think, the usual syndrome of the thankfulness and perhaps even awe of an amateur accepted by professionals — to some of whom he sometimes turned for advice or, rather, confirmation (unnecessary, to be sure) of the quality and value of his writings. However, that was one of the ways in which he was different from others at the Institute. Some of them mentioned to him how difficult it was to discipline themselves, to force themselves to begin writing. For Kennan *that* was no problem at all. He had to write.* He differed from the others in other ways too. An ivory tower mentality appealed to many of them, but not really to him. The preoccupations of some of them within their own fields of knowledge he found, rightly, too narrow and perhaps even petty. He was intellectual, rather than being An Intellectual; in the Institute he was something of a solitary patrician among groups of successful middle class.

He was aware, very much aware, of the responsibilities of this newly found freedom. I think he would have agreed with Aristotle that to be free may be more difficult than not to be free: but the routine of his life in Princeton was more than agreeable. He could, when he wanted, walk or bicycle from their house to the Institute in fifteen minutes or less. He was afforded intelligent secretaries who, as throughout his life, loved him and stayed with him for many long years. What was and remained difficult was the invasion of requests addressed to him, requests for lectures, solicitations for articles, for reading manuscripts, etc., etc. After all, he had become well known. He would, I think, have agreed with the wit who said that a celebrity is someone who is famous for being well known, and a celebrity he did not wish to be. Yet this inundation of requests, while a consequence of his public reputation, was after all due to his own concern with his country. That concern endured till the end. His conscience moved

* And not for financial reasons. He did not have to confront the dilemma formulated by Walter Scott: "Literature is a good staff; but a bad crutch."

and directed it. The result was an accumulation of statements, in various articles, books, recordings, interviews, speeches, addresses, that qualified him, at least in the eyes of some people, as a national treasure. Now allow me to suggest that he became even more than that: a conscience of a nation.

## 2

Let me now pause for a moment — since, after all, this book is a study of a man's character. We have now reached 1953, his fiftieth year. After that life may still bring changes and surprises and thus remain unpredictable: but a man's character changes hardly or not at all. And by "character" I mean his *conscious* decisions, choices, acts and words, but nothing of his — so-called — subconscious; that is, no attributions of psychoanalytic categories, no ham-handed projections or propositions of secret or hidden motives. Nor is there much sense to speculate when Kennan's character was definitely formed: in his twenties or thirties or forties? But, having arrived at 1953, I must draw readers' attention to an impressive and important trait of his character, which is the consistency of his mind. For by 1953 the consistency of his thinking and of his preferences began to be questioned by certain people; and occasionally, questions have been raised about it by various scholars ever since.

Putting the question as simply as possible: Kennan rose high, he became well known because of his stern and early anticommunism; he was an advocate of an energetic American stand against the Soviet Union; but now more and more of his ideas and utterances were directed against his nation's anticommunism. He was the architect of "Containment"; but had he now become an opponent of "Liberation"? Already by 1953 the first influential book attacking Kennan became current on the American market. Its title was *Containment or Liberation?*, its author was James Burnham, a pillar of the budding American "conservative" movement. Was Kennan a once conservative who had now turned liberal? Was he an American nationalist who turned internationalist? There were some people who thought so in 1953 — and then some more afterward. Such people, including some political scientists or historians of the Cold War, raised or suggested the question: were there two Kennans? Or, if not, did George Kennan change his mind? But there were not two George Kennans, and he had not changed his mind. As early as in 1946 there were instances when he warned not only against the then remnant American illusions about the Soviet Union but against the extremes of the ideology of anticommunism. Such statements he expressed frequently in succeeding years when the Cold War had begun. He warned against the militarization of "containment"; against the permanent establishment of American military bases in the middle of Europe and elsewhere on the globe; against going beyond the 38th parallel in Korea; against the encirclement of the Soviet Union and attempts to overthrow its government. But by 1953 his concerns about the dangerous applications and the popularity of an American anticommunist ideology had preoccupied his mind to an extent that they were greater than his erstwhile concerns about the dangers of communism and communists; and this went beyond his anxieties and advocacies about American foreign policy. He saw anticommunism becoming identical with American patriotism — or, indeed, substituting or even replacing the latter.

It would be quite wrong to attribute all this to a change of beliefs; and it would also be wrong to attribute this by saying that George Kennan was a moderate who did not like extreme doctrines. He himself said that Containment was not A Doctrine; that he had no doctrines, only principles. Now consider that principles and ideas are not the same. More than one hundred and fifty years ago Metternich wrote in a letter that while an idea is a fixed gun capable of striking error along one fixed line, a principle is like a gun mounted on a revolving platform, capable of striking error in any direction. Or consider again Edmund Burke, who supported the Americans in 1776 but was an adversary of the French revolutionaries in 1789, about whom John Morley wrote that Burke changed his aims but he never changed his stand. Or consider Churchill, whose character and temperament were very different from Kennan's but who, like Kennan, had a "curious courage before the convictions of others," who in 1945 was criticized by Americans (including General Eisenhower) of being dangerously anti-Soviet and who after 1950 was dismissed by Eisenhower and others for being dangerously pro-Soviet, perhaps even senile. Churchill's and Kennan's views of the world had much in common.

But we must go further than that. The consistency of Kennan's principles was part and parcel of his integrity. Here was a handsome and impressive man, still young, a superb speaker who awoke his nation about the dangers of communism, not a liberal internationalist, not one of the New Deal crowd: what a prospect of a public career stood before him in and after 1946! But that never tempted George Kennan, it never occurred to him — just as he never thought then, or even in retrospect after many years, that there was any inconsistency between his anticommunism and what may be called his anti-anticommunism.

By 1953 he knew that anticommunism was the greater danger.* But now there were more profound reasons for his anxiety, involving more than errors in the course of the foreign policy of his nation: he saw a corrosive addiction impairing the very vitals of his nation. The clearest and strongest expression of his concerns may be found in his address at the University of Notre Dame in 1953.† There he said, among other things:

> There are forces at large in our society today. . . . They all march, in one way or another, under the banner of an alarmed and exercized anti-communism. . . . I have the deepest misgivings about the direction and effects of their efforts. . . . They impel us — in the name of our salvation from the dangers of communism — to many of the habits of thought and action [of our Soviet adversaries]. . . . I tremble when I see this attempt to make a semi-religious cult out of emotional-political currents of the moment . . . designed to appeal only to men's capacity for hatred and fear, never to their capacity for forgiveness and charity and understanding. . . . Remember that the ultimate judgments of good and evil are not ours to make: that the wrath of man against his fellow man must always be tempered by the recollection of his weakness and fallibility and by the example of forgiveness and redemption which is the essence of his Christian heritage.

---

* Let me put it this way: the ideology of communism is the result of an idea of human nature and of history that is largely a lie (whence its incipient weaknesses); the ideology of anticommunism is a half-truth; and (again because of human nature) half-truths are more insidious and dangerous than are lies.

† Reprinted, in its entirety, in the Appendix, pages 192–200.

There was much more at stake here than foreign policy. Kennan's concerns were with nothing less than the mind and character of his native people.

Kennan spoke thus in public on 15 May 1953 — a month before his final departure from the Department of State, where he still had a desk and some work, and when President Eisenhower would still have him participate in the aforementioned Solarium conference. Thereafter Kennan's conscience moved him, again and again, to speak out against the misconceptions and misstatements and misdeeds of the American anticommunist "Right" — admittedly imprecise term though that is. This profoundly conservative and traditionalist American found that his worst adversaries were the American "conservatives" — an increasing mass with whom, by 1980, more Americans were willing to identify themselves than with "liberals." This was a landslide in American politics that still awaits a serious and reliable historian to analyze and limn it, but which is far beyond the scope of this chapter or book. Yet we must, at least for a moment, open our eyes and see how since about 1950 this development, seldom interrupted, advanced together with the popular belief of American omnipotence, with the spreading of hundreds of American military bases all around the world, with the willingness to employ American military power halfway across it, with the sense of an American hegemony, moving inexorably and with few interruptions from the presidencies of Eisenhower and Kennedy and Johnson and Nixon through Reagan and Clinton to George W. Bush. When the Soviet empire collapsed in 1989, people remembered and praised Kennan, who made it possible to "contain" the Soviet Union without war. There was some truth in this; but Kennan, more than ninety years old in the 1990s, could still witness a further and further American extension of military bases and alliances. Near the end of his life he still spoke out against these things, his last warnings that had accumulated during more than fifty years: a singular voice of a patriot, unknown by the vast majority of his people but still an American voice of conscience.

3

Still — there are dualities within every man, and so there were within George Kennan. Integrity does not mean rigidity, let alone singlemindedness; and conscience, every so often, involves an inner struggle within oneself. Through Kennan's life that struggle involved his patriotism with his pessimism. I wrote before that he was a patriot and not a nationalist: because patriotism is defensive, while nationalism is aggressive; because patriotism is traditionalist, while nationalism is populist; because patriotism is the love of one's land and of its history, while nationalism is a viscous cement that binds formless masses together. A patriot will be concerned with his nation's faults (Chesterton: "my country right or wrong is saying: my mother drunk or sober"). In Kennan's mind the river of pessimism ran very deep. Some of its evidences are there in the most startling pages of his diaries, some of them written at a time when his career was still at or near its peak. In 1949, for example, his bitterest descriptions are no longer those of shortsighted academics but of midwestern businessmen talking to each other on a train: he saw them, as he saw many Americans of that time, as caricatures. There is little charity in what he saw and was compelled to write down for himself; and yet his concern with such incarnations of

American character was, somehow, participant. They were no more or no less sincere than his, often also astonishing, expressions of humility and compassion.

On another, more mundane level we can see a duality of his conscious purposes, concerning his career. We have seen that his passage from official to unofficial, from a governmental to an intellectual career was a transition, from about 1950 to 1953. But during that time, even though his appointment to the Institute was already assured, there was his remnant wish that, after all, there might still be a suitable appointment in Washington for him, recognition of his talents. To say that he still wished "to serve his country" would be imprecise: he could, after all, serve his country unofficially, with his pen. But at the same time he was not devoid of some ambitions that were political. Eisenhower no longer continued to solicit his counsel; but he thought that he could be useful to Adlai Stevenson* around the next presidential election. More significant — and interesting — was a brief episode, probably in 1954, when, in response to some of his Pennsylvania farmer neighbors, he considered seriously to stand† for Congress as a Democrat in his southeastern Pennsylvania district. I write "probably in 1954" because, curiously, he suggests in his *Memoirs* the date for this as 1951: that remains for a future biographer to ascertain. He withdrew his candidacy (after thinking that he might cover its expenses himself) when he learned that his employment in the Institute and by the

---

* Stevenson was weak. When it was rumored that he was listening to Kennan, a Polish-American Democratic congressman admonished him not to rely on the latter, who was inclined to "appease" the Soviet Union. Thereafter Stevenson's connections with Kennan ceased.

† "Stand," not "run." George Kennan would not "run" for office . . .

Rockefeller Foundation prohibited support of candidates for public office.

Alfred Kazin wrote about the *Memoirs* in 1972 in the *New York Review of Books* that Kennan suffers "the futility of wanting to be nothing but an insider — while thinking like an outsider." This is too clever by half. Kennan never wanted to be an insider; he wanted not acceptance but influence. Nor did he really think as an "outsider": he knew that he was an outsider because of the independence of his mind, not the other way around.

The Kennans' life now divided between Princeton and the farm. He felt a kinship to some of the plain American men and women who worked there, especially to one of them, the part-time caretaker. He wrote about his daughter in his private diaries. More than thirty years later he chose to include some of this from the many thousands of pages of his accumulated diaries in a book, *Sketches from a Life*. For once I feel compelled to write something, ever so inadequately, not about his intellect but about his heart. Of course "mind" includes both brain and heart, much more interdependent as they are than modern intellectualism and psychology admit, but there it is, and there it is in a man whose reputation exists because of his intellectual powers; and yet how many of those qualities sprang from the tenderness of his heart! At least for this writer the deepest-felt pages in those self-selected fragments of his diaries are those that he wrote in July 1955, when he had gone back to Milwaukee for a few days. He went with his sister to find, after many years, the graves of his mother and of his father. He had not seen them before. The graves were not easy to find, but they found them. To his great relief his parents were buried next to each other. Reading his page about them one can, no, one must, feel a throb of one's emotions, a tremor behind one's eyes, sensing the pulsations of *his* heart right there in that cemetery — and simultaneously when what he wrote that evening on a desk or table somewhere in his sister's house; and, again simultaneously, sixty or more years later in the heart and behind the eyes of another distant human being reading that page. That "simultaneously" is a mystery. It is a mark of more than fine writing; it is an evocative achievement because of a great grave sweetness in the heart of a man. One year later he was back in Milwaukee again, to look at their old house and those two graves. He wept like a child. He felt no need to conceal that from his future readers.

During those years, 1953–56, there was another division of his labors. He accepted a number of invitations to lecture at universities (one of them, in 1954, at the University of Frankfurt, an early instance of the increasing reputation and respect he would have in Germany during the next fifty years). He wrote out his speeches, some of them soon reprinted as articles; he wrote other articles, the great majority of which dealt with public affairs, not only with foreign policy. At the same time he began to devote himself to something else: to the research and the writing of serious histories. There was one forerunner to that, his lectures on American diplomacy, 1900–1950, given at the University of Chicago in 1951, a brilliant essay. But now he turned to details and to varieties of research, resulting in the first volume of his *American-Soviet Relations, 1917–1920,* finished in early 1956 and published later in the same year. I shall devote a chapter to George Kennan the historian; here it is enough to note that after 1954 he divided his days between his two self-imposed tasks, that of becoming a serious historian and that of continuing a deeply concerned public writer and speaker.

What he had foreseen and what he had hoped to see was now happening: the postwar Soviet empire began to retreat. In 1954 and 1955 Stalin's successors chose to accept the neutrality of Austria and withdrew from the Russian zone there; they gave up the Russian bases in Finland; they abandoned their possessions on the China coast and in Manchuria; they renewed their relations with Yugoslavia; they recognized the West German government without insisting that the Western powers recognize the East German one, etc. Eisenhower and Dulles recognized the meaning of these steps not at all; they were indifferent to them and continued to expect nothing but, at best, a cold hostility between the United States and Russia. In February 1956 Khrushchev made a secret speech to the Twentieth Party Congress. He attacked Stalin's brutalities and crimes, "the cult of personality." That was a stunning development. Kennan saw it as yet another important symptom of the unease of the new rulers of the Soviet Union — an unease suggesting the prospect of significant changes in the condition of the Cold War. (He had recognized the rise of Khrushchev as early as in August 1952.) In July 1956 section nine of the Republican Party's platform called for nothing less than "the establishment of American air or naval bases all around the Soviet Union." In October 1956 the Russians came face to face with a political crisis in Poland, and immediately thereafter with a revolution in Hungary. Kennan thought and, on occasion, said that the Soviet empire in eastern Europe was cracking; that even after and despite the Russian military suppression of the revolt in Hungary, the Soviets would never recover.

That was not what Eisenhower or Dulles or indeed the overwhelming mass of American popular sentiment saw, or thought. But a few months later (after the public praise of his first history volume) Kennan took his opportunity to speak out about world affairs — in England.

4

He had been invited to accept a year's visiting professorship in Oxford. Early in 1957 there came another invitation: to give the important Reith Lectures (on six successive evenings, once a week), a principal program of the BBC in London.

He took this opportunity with avidity. Here was a chance to speak out, to express his gathering convictions and distilled concerns about the Cold War after a — relative — loneliness of three or four years. A change; and a challenge. The composition of his lectures was not difficult; circumstances and the conditions of his life in Oxford were. That famous town was a compound of what was admirable and old with what had become unattractive and new. So were their lodgings; so were their social surroundings, so typically English: a compound of thoughtful respect and of thoughtless inattention, of genuine hospitality and a no less genuine reserve. He felt this in Oxford, the, often physical, mixture of sunshine and clouds, of warmth and chill. Amazing, again, is the feverish energy of his writing and rewriting that he devoted to this task of the six lectures and the preparation for them. The Reith Lectures had a large audience: he also understood that, perhaps for the first time, not only his text but his diction had to be prepared carefully; that he would speak into a microphone alone, in an empty room in a studio. He had much to say: six lectures of thirty minutes; he must do this very well, and without the sense of reactions from an audience. When he first sat down before the microphone he was quite nervous. He need not have been. His audience was unusually large; and so was, unexpectedly, the worldwide reaction to what he said.

That worldwide reaction was mainly the result of two of these lectures, the third and the fourth ones, whose themes were (and had been, and would remain) the closest to Kennan's concerns. One dealt with the division of Europe and of Germany, the other with the question of nuclear weapons. Their essence may be summed up as follows. The division of Germany and of Europe was an absurd condition. Even the Russians must consider to change it. There were now signs of that too.* Yet there was no inclination to attempt negotiating with them about anything like that, no sign that the United States and the West would even consider doing so. Any withdrawal must be east of the iron curtain, none west of it. The American and the British and the French and the West German governments were satisfied with the division of Germany and Europe, though — hypocritically — they would not say so. About the matter of atomic or hydrogen weapons: the present American policy of "massive retaliation" was senseless. The most that must be said of these, in many ways, unusable weapons was that they must be kept in reserve. The West must commit itself to the principle of no first use; and the positioning of nuclear weapons in western Europe, including West Germany, was both dangerous and senseless.

What now followed, instantly, was an explosive reaction on both sides of the Atlantic. There were two reasons for that. One

---

* In 1957 that was detectable in some of Khrushchev's statements; and in the plan proposed by the Polish foreign minister Rapacki for a nonnuclear zone across all of central and some of eastern Europe, both west and east of the iron curtain.

was Kennan's prestige — at that time at least as wide in Britain as in the United States. That was of course inseparable from the measured calmness and lucidity of his arguments. The other reason was that his arguments were attractive and therefore at least potentially dangerous, especially in Germany. Consequently the reaction against Kennan's lectures was loud and harsh; and in some instances orchestrated. It included an unusually strong and ad hominem attack on Kennan from Acheson. Even more regrettable was the orchestrated rejection of Kennan by the Adenauer regime in West Germany and also by other German political figures. In Paris and in New York intellectual conventicles were organized, including famous scholars, for the purpose of declaring Kennan's ideas wrong. It was altogether an, in retrospect, lamentable but also expectable chorus of what the French call *les bien-pensants:* the "righteous thinkers."

On Kennan these effects were almost traumatic. Whether as a consquence or not, he was exhausted. He spent a few days in a hospital in Zurich. He had often respected the Swiss. On one occasion that year he jotted down in his diary that Switzerland and Finland were two European countries whose foreign policies were "the only sound and sensible ones in the world." There was now a tier of "neutral" states in Europe: Finland, Sweden, Switzerland, Austria, Yugoslavia (the latter in its own way), extending from north to south in the middle of Europe, separating the American and the Soviet military alliances — and, for God's sake, could that tier not expand in both directions, east and west, and — perhaps — include Germany too?

That would not happen. There were too many vested interests against that, and too many of their justifications by ideological categories. Kennan knew that. He also thought that, by 1957, his propositions might not have been timely enough. However, he was invited to speak to diverse audiences in Europe. During the next two years he traveled to France, Germany, Switzerland, Denmark, Norway, Austria, Italy, back to England on occasion. Meanwhile he finished the second volume of his magisterial *American-Soviet Relations, 1917–1920.* Other articles of his, including the texts of his Reith Lectures, were published in book form. Then came yet another change in his career.

5

One day in January 1961 John Kennedy, the newly elected president of the United States, had his telephone operator track down Kennan, who was at that time a one-semester visiting professor at Yale. The president asked him whether he would accept an appointment to become American ambassador either to Poland or to Yugoslavia. Kennan thanked the president. Later that day he answered him: he wished to be assigned to Yugoslavia.

It must not be thought that to Kennan this was a wholly unexpected surprise. Year after year he still hoped against hope that he might be called back to serve or counsel the government in one way or another. Was that the real motive of his many articles and lectures? No, because the motives and the purposes of men are seldom monocausal. Yet — as happens with anything in the history of ideas — ideas are, after all, inseparable from the person who chooses and then represents them. Kennan had taken it upon himself to send one or two of his writings, including the Reith Lectures in 1958 to John Kennedy, at that time a potential candidate for the presidency, to which Kennedy sent intelligent and cautious responses.* And, once Kennedy was elected, Kennan thought that he might receive some notice from the White House. He had reasons not to be pleased with Kennedy's selection of Dean Rusk for his secretary of state, a mediocre man who twelve years before had been mumbling his reservations to Kennan's propositions in the Policy Planning Staff. However, in January 1961 Kennan was grateful for and even happy with his new assignment. In fairly high spirits he sailed for Yugoslavia less than three months later with his family.

He was ambassador there for little more than two years. Perhaps he should have been given a more important position; but that would have somehow meant that the Kennedy administration identified itself with Kennan's so often contrarian views of what American policy should be: that would have been expecting too much. There was a particular reason why Kennan's assignment to Yugoslavia was apposite: in 1948 and 1949 his views and papers about how to handle Tito had been judicious and unexceptionable. In any event he liked his new situation in Belgrade. His ambassadorial actions and policies were accurate and proper. Also, as before in Russia, he developed an affection for the native peoples there. (I write "peoples" because he did not then foresee the violence and the depth of their ethnic differences and hostilities.) He also appreciated Tito's statesmanship, perhaps a bit beyond the latter's deserts. (Tito called him A Scholar.)

At the same time he was, as so often, vexed, to the extent of a

---

* Kennan had met John Kennedy once before, in 1939, when the latter, a callow youth then, was visiting Prague, going through Europe at the behest of his father, presenting himself at the American legation. Kennan, at that time, was irritated (to say the least) with such requests for attention, impositions on his time and his regular duties.

bitter grievance, with the irresponsible and ideological misdeeds of congressmen and of other pressure groups at home. In 1959 Congress, supported mostly by Republicans, declared a senseless and stupid Captive Nations Resolution, resulting, among other things, in a Captive Nations Day. The resolution attacked the Soviet Union proper (naming also nonexistent portions and imaginary peoples within it); and it also included Yugoslavia as a "captive nation." One result of this was to push the latter closer to the Soviet bloc (of which it had not been a member after 1948). Another was the protracted discrimination against Yugoslavia in American trade policies. Kennan traveled back to Washington to talk to important congressmen about this, but to no avail. Kennedy did not much support his ambassador about these matters. The result was a typical Kennan reaction: he would resign his ambassadorship in order to return to academic life a year before the completion of his customary three-year term.

He was still in Belgrade during the Cuban missile crisis. We do not know what he thought then; but we may assume that he was not especially agitated (as were Rusk and Acheson and many others). He did not think that Russia would risk a nuclear war for the sake of Cuba (just as the United States did not, in 1956, consider anything like that for the sake of Hungary). He did not know then — but he would learn later — Kennedy's decision, kept secret from the American people, to withdraw American rocket bases from Turkey in exchange for the removal of such Russian armaments in Cuba. Kennan would have approved of that: that was, after all, a reciprocal disengagement of American and Russian military bases somewhere on the globe. A few months after he came home from Belgrade he was irritated when Rusk, without having consulted him, suddenly chose to invite Tito to a state visit in the United States (which was then marred by hostile demonstrations by ethnic groups). That occurred a month before John Kennedy was shot dead.*

Such was the end of George Kennan's services to his government. He was grateful for that last opportunity, given to him by a president whom he esteemed. He was moved to write a fulsome note to Kennedy, who wrote back to Kennan: "It is a great encouragement to have the support of a diplomat and historian of your quality." It is pleasant to record Kennedy's esteem of Kennan the historian now, when his diplomatic career was finally over but when some of his finest history writing was yet to come.

6

In this book I shall devote a chapter to George Kennan's historianship, departing from the expectable chronological account of his life. There we shall see that he wrote his first history, a wideranging and profound essay, in 1950; and that he finished his last history, a contemplative narrative of his ancestors, in 2000, in the ninety-seventh year of his life. But now, coming back to the main story of his life, we must recognize the two milestones of 1963 and 1988: the first the end of his last public office, the second: *his* end of the Cold War. And that was a very active quarter-century of his life, full of achievements to which I must now turn.

---

* It is interesting (there is no evidence for this except a somewhat cryptic footnote in his *Memoirs*) that Kennan was not satisfied with all of the conclusions of the otherwise proper Warren Commission investigating Kennedy's assassination in Dallas and subsequent events — because of unanswered questions about Jack Ruby and of the latter's and Oswald's connections with American clandestine service, including the CIA.

His health was now quite good. He had been beset with various illnesses during his youth and then even in his fifties. But, except for troubles with his knees, beginning at eighty, he was hale, spare, strong, well beyond the expectable standards of his age.* At the age of seventy-four he sailed in his small boat with his wife and brother-in-law from Stockholm to their house in Norway, about seven hundred miles in those, seldom calm, Baltic and northern seas: he called it their "geriatric cruise." (The previous summer they had sailed to Stockholm.) This was the second sailboat he had bought, equipped with a small auxiliary motor. He had now sufficient income from royalties and lectures to afford something like that: never rich but comfortable enough.

During those twenty-five years he traveled much, almost always with his wife. He kept writing his diaries. He abhorred the cramped and herded conditions of air travel. Yet it was not until almost the age of ninety that his transoceanic traveling diminished, and even then not entirely so. Within the United States they traveled till almost the ninety-ninth year of his life.† In the mid-1960s he flew to lecture in Japan; in 1980 to China. They visited South Africa three times. Twenty years after he had been forbidden to return to Moscow he returned to Russia in 1973, to Leningrad; in 1976 to ports on the Black Sea. There were many other journeys in Europe connected with his researches, espe-

---

* His tendency for pessimism appeared from time to time when he would say to his family and friends that he was close to the end of his life when that was not so.

† One memorable occasion, among many lectures, was his visit in 1968 to Ripon College in Wisconsin, where he received an honorary doctorate, sixty years after his father had been honored there.

cially in Vienna, Berlin, Paris. In 1986 they went to Budapest for the sake of a cure of his knees in the thermal baths there. He wrote one of his most poignant and history-laden "reflections" about Leningrad in a long essay printed in the *New Yorker* in 1974. Reading that one gets the sense how he foresaw the end of the Cold War (and perhaps even the approaching end of the Soviet system) a good fifteen years before that would come about. In 1981 and 1984 he went to Moscow, in 1987 to Moscow and Riga, revisiting and musing about places and houses he had known fifty or more years before. By then he more than foresaw, he *knew* that the Soviet system in Russia and the Cold War between America and Russia had ended. In late 1987 he gave a brief interview to a small American magazine* entitled "Obituary for the Cold War." This was two years before the fall of the Berlin Wall (unforeseen and unexpected by the Central Intelligence Agency and other agencies in Washington), and four years before the dissolution of the Soviet Union.

There was one partial change of the Kennans' habitations after the sixtieth year of their life. The small seaside house in Kristiansand, Norway, which belonged to his wife's family (and where he had met them in 1931, asking for their daughter's hand), now became their summer home. They spent almost every summer there, about six weeks in July and August, the last time in the ninety-eighth year of his life. That also led to his buying and sailing a boat.† Here, too, something may be said about the dualities of his thoughts. He was very much at home with his

---

* *New Perspectives,* published in their Summer 1988 number.
† Is it — perhaps — significant that he christened his first boat *Nagawicka* after a river of Wisconsin; and the second *Northwind* ?

wife's family in Norway; but he also thought that he was a foreigner there. That did not mean that he was anxious to return to Princeton; his mind (and his hands) were sufficiently busy in Kristiansand. But his pessimism about what was happening in the world, and to civilization, affected him there too. He was critical of the behavior of young Scandinavians and of modern welfare states. On one occasion he wrote that the ideal, "I fear, European or American, is not that more people should live really well, but that no one should." Yet he recognized that this condemnation may have been too harsh. Much later, responding to this writer, he agreed that, beneath all of that economic and political socialism, there was a deep bourgeois stratum of life and of standards among Scandinavian peoples that was as valuable and perhaps even more enduring than almost anywhere else in Europe and in the world.

He and his wife now visited their farm less often. In 1976 they gave it to their second daughter Joan, who lived in Washington with her husband. Nineteen eighty-nine was of course a milestone, because of the end of the Cold War that not only made his reputation but that framed his years and was the main subject of his concerns.* But 1989 was a milestone in an even larger sense. He saw, as early as 1989, that more than the Cold War had ended: what was coming to end was the entire twentieth century, a short century that began in 1914 and that was formed by World War I and World War II and the Cold War, each largely the consequence of the other. He was a member, and a witness,

---

* This is not the place to list his many encomia. They included a number of national (and German) book awards and prizes and government decorations, the foundation of a Kennan Institute of Advanced Russian Studies, the Presidential Medal of Freedom in 1989.

and a participant of that century, living through and even after it. The causes and the consequences of its tragedies preoccupied him, inspiring him to write his articles and his histories, on many occasions well after 1989 and devoted to subjects well before the Cold War and even before 1914. That was why 1989 was a milestone but not a turning point of his life. He saw that the Cold War was a consequence, not a cause; he was convinced that the great catastrophic event of his century was not 1917, not the Russian revolution,* no matter how much and how profound his knowledge of that was. It was 1914, the outbreak of the First World War in Europe, to the history of the origins and the causes of which he devoted so much of his energies before 1989, and whose consequences would still preoccupy him.

His tasks were self-imposed. They were multiple and multifarious. Their evidences are there in the mass of his diaries and letters and his publications, especially during that quarter-century. Besides his correspondences there are his memoirs, histories, books with other themes, yet others containing some of his travel diaries, again others containing collected and coherent lectures and/or articles of his about a single theme; printed interviews, book reviews, reprints, letters to editors, and others. There exists, as yet, no complete list of his published writings — I dare to say that even in this era of computerized data, a mere listing of them would be difficult, if not impossible, to compile without omissions or other errors.† Until the forty-fourth year

---

*To most American "conservatives" it *was* the communist revolution in 1917; as William F. Buckley and James Burnham wrote: "In 1917 history changed gears."
†*George F. Kennan: An Annotated Bibliography* was published in 1997 by

of his life he wrote to and for his government. (There may have been only two exceptions: a short article in 1942 for the *American Foreign Service Journal* about the remaining Americans' internment in Germany, and another article that he wrote [in German!] in 1927 or 1928, published in a German newspaper, when and where I do not know.) Now he began to write to and for the American public. In the ten years from 1953 to 1963 he wrote at least fifty serious articles (in 1959 alone perhaps as many as fifteen); during the quarter-century from 1963 to 1989 at least six dozen. He did not stop writing for the public until the ninety-eighth year of his life. (He wrote or dictated letters to his friends until the ninety-ninth.)

What did he write about? What did he wish to admonish, to remind, to warn against? The Cold War, of course: but that is an inadequate summary: about what his country, its government, and its people ought to do or not to do; what and how they ought to see and to think. His themes and subjects were never repetitious, because the world was changing and the Cold War itself was changing, and because of the clarity and the independence of his mind. Here I can but list shorthand and inadequate summaries of his concerns. He opposed the American war in Vietnam: because he was convinced that there was no need for an American military presence in that portion of Asia; because he saw that what had risen there was not anything like international communism but yet another Asian kind of nationalism; because

---

Greenwood Press. Written by Laurel B. Franklin, the annotations are thoughtful and intelligent; but even this very valuable guide could not be complete.

the Soviet Union was not at all involved in Indochina. And behind that stood a larger and greater issue: Russia and China. Earlier than perhaps anyone else Kennan saw and spoke and wrote about the apparent differences and potential conflicts between Russia and China, whether communist or not; and that America's relations with Russia were more important than America's relations with China. Now he could witness, especially after 1971, the American preference for China; he was, again, alone in thinking and, on occasion, saying that the opposite of that should have been and should be the American choice. When in the 1970s relations with Russia were somewhat improving and the word "détente" had become current, he warned that this was not enough; that the Soviet Union had begun to change and crack and creak; that, among other matters, the American insistence that the Soviet Union facilitate emigration of its citizens in accord with some American preferences was entirely wrong. Then came the American support for and shipment of weapons to Afghan tribesmen fighting Russians; the chief foreign policy adviser of a president photographed on the Afghan border sporting a submachine gun; Ronald Reagan and his "Evil Empire," and so on. But then came the ending of the Soviet empire in eastern Europe, the end of communism within Russia itself, the end of the Cold War—a surprise to most Americans, including their government, though not to George Kennan.

Several times during that quarter-century he appeared, too, before the Senate Committee on Foreign Relations, where he was received and heard with respect, but with little or no effects. He met and helped Stalin's daughter Svetlana when she had fled Russia and come to the United States; he helped and supported

Alexander Solzhenitsyn, the significance of whose books and of his expulsion from the Soviet Union he instantly recognized. (Thereafter Solzhenitsyn would criticize him, but that is another story.) But, beyond the Cold War, he wrote and warned, with utmost seriousness, against the armament race and nuclear weapons. He knew that armaments were results and not causes of conflicts between states: but also that the very existence of nuclear weapons elevated dangers of mankind to hitherto unprecedented levels. He made numberless speeches and wrote numberless articles about this grim topic, and an entire book, *The Nuclear Delusion: Soviet-American Relations in the Nuclear Age.* About these dangers, and in his advocacy of nuclear disarmament, he was not alone: but, again and again, his advice and his reasoning were unique.* It is symptomatic that four-fifths of this book deals with American-Soviet relations. His last essay in this book, written in 1982, bears the title: "A Christian's View of the Arms Race." At the very end of this he wrote: "The readiness to use nuclear weapons against other human beings — against people whom we do not know, whom we have never seen, and whose guilt or innocence is not for us to establish — this is noth-

---

* It may be noteworthy that he began this volume with a poem by the American poet Richard Wilbur. "Advice to a Prophet," its first stanzas:

When you come, as you soon must, to the streets of our city,
Mad-eyed from stating the obvious,
Not proclaiming our fall but begging us
In God's name to have self-pity,

Spare us all word of the weapons, their force and range,
The long numbers that rocket the mind;
Our slow, unreckoning hearts will be left behind,
Unable to fear what is too strange.

ing less than a presumption, a blasphemy, an indignity — an indignity of monstrous dimensions — offered to God!"

That exclamation mark — so unusual, so poignant (in the literal sense of that word) was his.

Then came the — providential — unpredictability of history (including the unpredictability of Russians). That the Soviet order was shaky, that Soviet rule in eastern Europe was beginning to crumble, that the ideology of communism was disappearing within Russia itself, Kennan knew — well enough to have been able to recognize its symptoms earlier than almost anyone else. As early as in 1985 he said (to me) that this man Gorbachev had begun to dismantle the Soviet Union. Two years later, during Gorbachev's visit to Washington in December 1987, he received an invitation to the Soviet embassy. His wife adminished him not to adopt his customary shyness and seek refuge from the crowd standing back against a wall. Mikhail Gorbachev, the head of the Soviet Union, recognized him. He grasped Kennan's elbow, looked in his eyes, and said: "Mr. Kennan. We in our country believe that a man may be a friend of another country and remain, at the same time, a loyal and devoted citizen of his own; and that is the way we view you."

That was George Kennan's apotheosis. The Cold War was over. Soon there came a public murmur of recognition. The author of "containment" had been right. But we shall see that God gave him yet more years to live, during which he did not cease to speak and write — because his concerns were, and remained, broader and deeper than the Cold War. Gorbachev may not have known how right he was when, in those words, he spoke of "a loyal and devoted citizen of his own." Yes, Kennan knew Russia; he understood Russia; he was attracted to Russia. But his main preoccupation has been with his own country. Yes: America's relations with Russia; but underneath it and above it, America's relationship with itself.

That was — and remained — both cause and result of his loneliness. That loneliness is why "the conscience of America," to adorn him with such an epithet, may be exaggerated. Among the 245 million Americans in 1989 how many knew his name? Perhaps one percent, perhaps even fewer. How many of that one percent ever heard his voice? How many read his writings? That mountain of dozens of books and hundreds of articles? Most of the latter appeared in no other than two or three publications. Well, they *were* printed, readers will say. He was, after all, known to America's intellectuals and academics; and were many great writers and thinkers ever read during their lifetime but by a few? Ah! but George Kennan was a lone — and often misunderstood — figure even in the eyes of some of those, too, who read him. I do not write "among intellectuals" because he was really not one of them — except sometimes at his single luncheon table in the cafeteria of the Institute at Princeton. "Conservative" publicists and writers — with very few honorable exceptions — kept assailing, dismissing, ignoring him. "Liberals" respected him when they shared his opposition to this or that war: but few of them really understood him, and at least some of them were uneasy with his past or present views about Germany or the Middle East or religion or the excrescences of liberalism. Kennan was right, by and large, about the Cold War: let that be; but that was all.

And yet — he wrote about the Cold War because in his nation's behavior and in his people's ideas he saw what was his deep and lasting concern with the fault lines and with the fragility of American civilization. For, just as the most telling (and often the only visible) marks of a man's character appear in his relationship with other human beings,* a nation's character often reveals itself clearest when it comes to its relations, to its behavior with other nations and peoples, something that goes beneath the category of "foreign relations." Unlike many Americans, George Kennan did not believe that the United States was A Chosen Nation of God, that its people were A Chosen People, or even the Last Best Hope of Mankind; but he believed that there is something unique in the history of every nation, including his own; and that the Cold War, though it had not been started by the United States, revealed some of the unhappy traits of the American mind: a willful ignorance beneath which there was something worse, a kind of national self-adulation. He also knew, and deeply felt, that the United States belonged within Western Civilization as did Europe (again, it was his respect for the inevitability of America's connection with Europe that many American "conservatives" as well as some American "liberals" did not share). His head and heart were aggrieved when he witnessed the fast dissolving civility in American lives, American manners, American mores (together with the hideous spreading of pornography). In the 1960s and in 1970 he spoke out seriously and scathingly against the repugnant acts and false standards of the "youth rebellion." These hordes of students were rebels without a program, he said publicly (and was of course misunderstood). His anguished warnings against nuclear armaments and their prospects were allied

---

*Every man has a relation with God, with himself, with other living beings, and with other human beings. The last two we can observe; the first two we may but surmise.

with his committed belief in conservation, for the preservation of land and of its resources. It is thus that we may detect principal inclinations of his mind. Those who respected him understood that he was a traditionalist. True: but there was more to that. He was not a Progressive. He believed that people, and especially Americans, have reached a time when they must rethink and revise the entire idea of "progress." That alone may — I shall not say that it will — qualify him as more than an intellectual, more than a conservative, more than a traditionalist: a lone voice of prophet, a conscience of his nation.

One day — not now — when in the midst of a world ruled by Mechanism the last vestiges of the old humanism will have vanished, a few, young rather than old, American men or women will stare at his words and see — rather than recognize — that this man was, once, a conscience of America. "A civilization disappears with the kind of man, the type of humanity, that has issued from it."* Yes, civilization may disappear, but not conscience. These future readers will be the repositories of conscience in a remnant America then. A few of them — but that is always so.

* Georges Bernanos.

# The Historian

I

Before I turn to the last chapter of George Kennan's life, I wish to draw attention to another of his achievements, to Kennan the historian. Readers patient enough to have followed the chapters till now will recognize that his thinking was saturated with history, that his respect for history was allied to that exceptional kind of nostalgia that involves a respectful longing for times and places well before one's childhood or youth.* However — such a taste for history does not necessarily result in an attempt to write

---

* Cf. Johan Huizinga: "A feeling of immediate contact with the past is a sensation as deep as the purest enjoyment of art; it is an almost ecstatic sensation of no longer being myself, of overflowing into the world around me, of touching the essence of things, of through history experiencing the truth. . . . The historic sensation is not the sensation of living the past again but of understanding the world [perhaps] as one does when listening to music. . . ."

it, just as a gourmet is not necessarily a cook (and a mental appetite for history is something else than intellectual gourmandise). But, beginning in 1950 — in the midst of the turmoil of his life and career, and beset with so many duties — George Kennan took up another self-imposed task: that of writing history, something that, with interruptions, and turning from theme to theme, topic to topic, he continued until the very last years of his life. Such were the inclinations and the powers of his mind.

The first such book, *American Diplomacy, 1900–1950,* may be his best-known one, having been assigned reading in many college and university courses soon after its appearance. It consisted of six lectures written and then delivered at the University of Chicago in the spring of 1951. Their structure, method, language, and purpose echo its author's principal and enduring preoccupations, expressed in so many of his lectures and articles. Coherent as many of those lectures and articles were, they could be put together in books; such volumes by Kennan were later published. But *American Diplomacy, 1900–1950* was different. It was Kennan's first attempt to write a history. More precisely: those Chicago lectures form one grand historical essay.

He stated his purpose at the very beginning. "I would like to say a word about the concept of these six lectures. The concept stems from no abstract interest in history for history's sake. It stems from a preoccupation with the problems of foreign policy we have before us today." In other words: writing about the past for the sake of the present. That is not "pure" history — but, then, "pure" history? Is there such a thing at all? The purpose of any and every history book in its writer's mind is never simple; but in this case at least Kennan's main purpose is easily detectable. It was educational.

This appeared from the above-cited first short paragraph of his first chapter to the concluding sixth chapter, entitled "Diplomacy in the Modern World"; but in their way the other five chapters, or lectures, were dedicated to that too. Their theme was, by and large, that of the repeated shortcomings of the conduct of foreign policy, particularly of American foreign policy, by and within a democracy. But there is more in this short book than admonition or exhortation. The contents of its five main chapters reveal a stunning amount of historical knowledge, and of historical insights. What Kennan must have read before and during his writing of these chapters is amazing* — perhaps especially as we keep in mind the wearisome and agitated conditions of his life in the months before and during their composition.

The successive chapters of *American Diplomacy, 1900–1950* are: "The War with Spain"; "The Origin of John Hay's Open Door"; "America and the Orient"; "World War I"; "World War II"; and the concluding summary and admonitory chapter. Students and established scholars of each of these important topics would, even now, profit from a quick rereading of these essays written more than a half-century ago. The 1898 war with Spain could have been avoided, and how easily; the American occupation and incorporation of the Philippines, of Puerto Rico, of Guam,

---

* One example. He began one of his chapters with a quotation from a then recent article by the British historian Herbert Butterfield that had appeared in the estimable but far from widely known (even by American academics) periodical *Review of Politics* (Notre Dame) in April 1950. Perhaps Kennan's was an example of the condensed wisdom that Jacob Burckhardt told his few students in Basel of what a student of history must do: nothing else but *Bisogna saper leggere:* you must know how to read (not merely "what" but "how").

etc., were unnecessary; they came about almost by accident. In 1900 John Hay's proclamation of an Open Door policy in China was the outcome of another odd coincidence; the protracted American illusions about China and a consequent conflict with Japan were not unavoidable. World War I was the greatest catastrophe of Western Civilization, which the United States should have recognized earlier — and in different ways — than it did. World War II was freighted with disaster, since the Western democracies from its very beginning could not defeat Germany without Soviet Russia. These are not summaries of his chapters; they are, rather, those of his insights. His anxious convictions shine through them, again and again. "I am talking about the behavior of the United States of America. History does not forgive us our national mistakes because they are explicable in terms of our domestic politics." "If it was the workings of our democracy that were inadequate in the past, let us say so." George Kennan was skeptical, indeed, pessimistic about many of the workings of democracy. Yet this book is not the work of an aristocratic critic of it. "I also suspect that what purports to be public opinion in most countries that consider themselves to have popular government is often not really the consensus of the feelings of the mass of the people at all but rather the expression of the interests of special highly vocal minorities."

It is in the last, admonitory, chapter that Kennan employed an argument and a term with which he became soon thereafter identified. Until this concluding chapter his concern was the damnable subordination of foreign policy — of the course of the ship of state — to calculations of domestic politics: to the floating sentiments of its crew and passengers. But now, at the end, he turns to those who are setting the course, to the inclinations and habits of their minds. "I see the most serious fault of our past policy formulation to lie in something that I might call the legalistic-moralistic approach to international problems. This approach runs like a red skein through our foreign policy of the last fifty years." And this is no longer the danger of democratic populism; it comes not from demagoguery but from abstraction. "The association of legalistic ideas with moralistic ones" is not an outcome of vulgarity but of a whitened sepulchral unreality—of an ideology characteristic of New England minds. This last attribution is mine, not Kennan's, and it is applicable to many kinds of Americans whose provenance was far away from Boston, but whose mindset depended on an insubstantial and legalistic ethicism of the kind of which perhaps Woodrow Wilson was a most typical representative. Beliefs in world law, the outlawing of war, Leagues of Nations, United Nations, World Government, etc., are, all, outcomes of that—as is their consequence of "total war" against "Evil." Here was (and remains) another potential for misunderstanding Kennan. From then on scholars and students of American foreign policy were wont to contrast Kennan "the realist" to the "idealist" category of American foreign policy-makers. One half of that fixation is correct but the other half not. "Moral" and "ethical" are not quite the same things. Perhaps he should have coined the term "legal-ethical" or "legalistic-moralizing" rather than "legalistic-moralistic," but that is not the main issue. Kennan's view of foreign policy and of the world and indeed of human nature was a moral one. And the American predicament, to this day, is the failure to understand that the opposite of idealism is materialism, not realism; indeed, that idealism and realism are the best possible combination; that history is made by what people think and believe and that the entire material organization of the world is but the superstructure, a consequence of that.

## 2

Future biographers will have to determine when George Kennan turned to his writing of a monumental and magisterial and massive history of Soviet-American relations from 1917 to 1920. It could not have occurred much earlier than sometime in 1954. That achievement is astonishing again. In less than four years Kennan wrote two large volumes, each more than five hundred pages long — four years during which his time and attention were diverted from that task again and again, to dozens of lectures (which he always wrote out with great care), articles, and other public duties, including the extraordinarily onerous preparation for delivering the Reith Lectures in 1957. But now his composing an exhaustive history, dependent on a very large amount of research, in accord with the practices (the proper term is "practices" rather than "method") of professional history, was something new. He knew that. He sought encouragement from a few men in the Institute that he then handsomely acknowledged in his preface. His relative freedom to read and work at the Institute and the devoted and intelligent assistance of his then secretary, Dorothy Hessman, were of course great help. Yet I find it difficult to imagine any professional historian capable of writing two such histories of a most complicated time and place and people, of exhausting masses of papers and materials in at least three languages, and fulfilling the requirements of scholarly and bibliographical practices to the last jot and tittle, indeed, in places beyond all expectable requirements.*

*Russia Leaves the War* is Kennan's historical reconstruction of American relations with Russia from the Bolshevik revolution in November 1917 to the Soviets' ratification of their treaty with Germany and the Central Powers at Brest-Litovsk in March 1918. It is a history of complicated entanglements for many reasons and on multiple levels. The United States kept its embassy and its consulates in Russia, when necessary, in contact with the new Soviet rulers, while Russia was still represented in Washington by a competent and intelligent ambassador appointed by the previous Russian government. There were other, different American missions in Russia, including the Red Cross, whose principal representative, Raymond Robins, was willing to maintain and extend his contacts with the Bolsheviks, giving them the benefit of doubt. The main American (and Allied) concern was to keep Russia in the war against the Germans somehow, since with Russia out of the war the Germans might win their decisive victory in France before or even despite the arrival of a large American army there. Kennan's acquaintance with and use of the various sources of these entanglements are exemplary. But the qualities of this book are more remarkable than this accomplishment of a specialized study. His unique and nonacademic insights appear at the very beginning, for his purpose in writing this book goes beyond that of academic readership, written only

---

* One example. During the writing of his book in 1955 Kennan found time and effort to compose a scholarly article on the so-called Sisson Documents, published in the *Journal of Modern History* in June 1956: an example not only of the assiduity of his research but of his wish to publish in a scholarly article results of his studies before publication of his book.

or even especially for other historians. The book begins with his description of the immediate background and of the personalities involved. His sketches of their characters are superb.* They are also compassionate and kind, even including those of men with whom Kennan disagrees.

There is a sense of purpose in these two volumes that are more than academic; they are instructive and educational. Thus, for example, one of his remarks about Woodrow Wilson, who, a few months before the Bolshevik revolution, declared that Russia was "a fit partner for a league of honor."† One can also find Kennan's throwaway maxims and insights within footnotes (as on the bottom of page 13: "that curious law which so often makes Americans, inveterately conservative at home, the partisans for radical change everywhere else"). Other footnotes (for

---

* Consider his portrait of Raymond Robins (who figures again and again in his two books). "Robins was a characteristic figure of the liberal movement of the Middle West in the years before World War I. As such, he shared in both the strengths and the weaknesses of that social phenomenon. He was supported by his capacity for enthusiasm, its sincerity, its robust confidence, its romanticism, and its love of action; but he suffered from its essential provincialism, the shallowness of its historical perspective, the erratic and unbalanced quality of many of its intellectual approaches. It was from this background that he derived his religious fervor and his faith in human progress; but it was also from this background that he derived that lack of roundedness, of tolerance, and of patience with the sad necessities of man's political existence which was to make his career as a figure in Russian-American relations so stormy, so episodic, and in the end so tragic."

†"The gap in understanding was greater, the measure of tragedy more profound, and the hour later than Wilson suspected. Pleasant words from a prosperous, well-meaning, and idealistic people, in whose mental world the profile of genuine human evil and passion had passed halfway into forgetfulness, could not penetrate the seething maelstrom of Russia, where the fabric of society had now been broken. . . . "

example, note 21 at the bottom of page 300) reveal his indefatigable research for the provenance of sources for French and Japanese documents.

*Russia Leaves the War* was a success. It received public prizes and the praise of historians. Of course Kennan was pleased with the approval. But he did not consider himself as an academic historian — or, rather, he was not so considered by many in the guild of the latter. The case of the Sisson Documents may be telling as well as amusing. Edgar Sisson was a newspaperman and editor and a representative of Wilson's Committee of Public Information in Russia. In February 1918 he received a stack of documents from a Russian, purporting to be evidence that Lenin and the Bolsheviks were financed, if not altogether employed, by the German government. Sisson, not without difficulty, carried these secret documents out of Russia. Thereafter they were widely publicized in the United States. To confirm their authenticity Wilson's Committee of Public Information appointed a committee of the National Board of Historical Research to examine them. That committee was composed by two of the most eminent American historians of that time. They pronounced: "We have no hesitation in declaring that we see no reason to doubt the genuineness or authenticity of these 53 [out of 68] documents." Thirty-seven years later Kennan wrote that "these documents were unquestionable forgeries from beginning to end."

Two years later *The Decision to Intervene* was published, another masterful and monumental volume dealing with not more than five months of Soviet-American relations. Here and there the reader may find that some of the material overlaps the first book; but, again, his approach is unique. The book begins with a powerful (and scathing) portrait of American (mostly East Coast) public opinion and its near-hysterical excesses in early 1918, amounting to a sociographic analysis of its acts and sentiments at that time, concluding with a rueful Kennanesque suggestion: "Perhaps it was partly in the subconscious effort to assure themselves of the reality of war that Americans gave themselves so prodigally to the external manifestations of the martial spirit." More in this volume than in the first there is Kennan's, perhaps old-fashioned but certainly traditional as well as practical, emphasis on the importance of the relations between governments. He, who had no sympathy with and no illusions about the Bolsheviks, still had an understanding for the efforts of those Americans such as Robins who worked for maintaining American relations with the Soviets, including Lenin and Trotsky. But he also believed that these efforts ought to have been coordinated with and subordinated to American official diplomacy. It is telling that he dedicated this book to two American consuls who had been toiling away in Moscow. "To the memory of two members of America's Foreign Service, De Witt Clinton Poole and Madden Summers, of whose faithful and distinguished efforts in Russia in their country's behalf this volume gives only an incomplete account." Elsewhere, in the same volume, he attributes to Summers's and Poole's adversary Robins "a dignity" worth recording and remembering. And then, here and there, Kennan interrupts his disentangling of the, worse than Gordian, knot of Russian-American relations with a clear vision of the future: yes, respect may be due to the illusions and ideals not only of Wilson but also of Lenin; but "the expectations of both were to be shattered by the experience of the succeeding decades, in which nationalism would emerge, to the surprise of great many people, as a political force far stronger than class feeling."

Sometime in July 1918 President Wilson decided (also because of pressures from the Allies) to send a small American force to land in the far north of Russia. This indecisive and ineffective intervention in what was — though only in some ways — a Russian civil war was a great mistake, both in the long and the short run: for at the very time of this limited landing the last great German offensive in France had been broken and the end of the war in Europe was coming into sight. These landings in Russia were thus as untimely as they were ineffective. Kennan traced their origins as well as he could. Yet, he wrote, in the end he could do no more "within the limits of a study intended to hold meaning for the general public as well as for the specialist." (Note again Kennan's dual aim: for whom he is writing.) "One encounters, at this point, the problem that is bound to beset diplomatic historians in increasing measure as they move into the effort to recount the course of the international life of the present century; the huge number and complexity of contrasts between the bloated governmental bureaucracies and the stupendous volume of the written record to which they have given rise. In these circumstances it becomes simply unfeasible to attempt to permit the sources to tell their own story. The historian has no choice but to simplify, to generalize, and to ask the reader to lean on his judgment." Here, as a newcomer to the profession, Kennan recognized something that many academic historians, alas, have failed to admit ever since.

Kennan ended his two-volume classic with the departure of the last American official representatives in Soviet Russia and with an impressionist description of their forlorn passage into Finland in October 1918. His previously announced plan to write the history of Soviet-American relations from 1917 to 1920 stopped there. Yet these relations, though no longer governmental or official, continued after October 1918, on different levels and in many instances, of which the most interesting were those in the Russian Far East, including an American naval and military presence in and around Vladivostok. But — we do not know when and why — Kennan chose not to write such a third and concluding volume about 1918–20, just as twenty years later he chose not to write a third after his two great volumes of European diplomatic history before 1914.

### 3

In 1961 was published *Russia and the West Under Lenin and Stalin*. Most of it consisted of or was drawn from lectures that Kennan had delivered to students at Oxford and then at Harvard. We have seen that his 1957 Reith Lectures were also put together in a book, but this one was different: a history not in the least ephemeral, and amounting to more than to a series of lectures. In this respect it was similar to his Chicago book in 1951; but in *Russia and the West Under Lenin and Stalin* the successive chapters do not consist of separate episodes in international history. Its substance is such that one who does not know the provenance of its chapters would be surprised to learn that they were successive lectures. Kennan's purpose was naturally educational; but the results soar beyond any imagined classroom. It is not a specialized study but something between a sweeping history and an excellent historical essay. Its worth endures after more than forty years; it contains almost nothing that requires correction because of other works and documents available ever since.*

There is, however, a connection between *Russia and the West Under Lenin and Stalin* and *The Decision to Intervene,* written and published three years earlier. A large portion of the later book, close to one half of it, deals with the Soviets' relations with the West from 1918 to 1921 — materials that would have provided the substance of a third volume of *Soviet-American Relations, 1917–1920* that Kennan had not written. There are also quotations, citations, remarks that had first appeared in the two published volumes. But there is nothing repetitious in this book. One of his virtues is Kennan's courage to write that, after all that is known and said about them, both Stalin and Hitler possessed the abilities of statesmanship.† I have only two caveats about Kennan's judgments — judgments as they are, rather than historical errors. One is his insistence that the Soviet Union was not "fit" to be an ally of the West after Hitler invaded it; that military and other help should have been given to Stalin, but only inasmuch and as long as the United States and Britain decided that to be useful; and that Stalin ought to have been told of that condition in so

---

* One stunning example of Kennan's insight (if that is what that was). On page 252 he writes, very briefly, of Stalin's sudden collapse in late June 1941, about a week after the German invasion of Russia on the 22nd: "quite paralyzed and helpless, lost his nerve, and had to be bailed out by the men around him." Yet what happened to Stalin on 28–30 June 1941 was not revealed by the reminiscences of Politburo members until the 1990s. Did Kennan surmise this thirty years earlier?

† For example, about Hitler (page 335): "a dangerous man, fanatical, brutal, unreliable. . . . But he was by no means a mountebank; and if it be conceded that evil can be great, then the quality of greatness cannot, I think, be denied to him."

many words. Kennan insisted on this idea, or thesis, throughout his life. He was unwilling to concede its impracticality, to recognize how much and how badly and to what extent the United States and Britain depended on Russia's participation in the world war against Germany. His other arguable judgment concerned Poland, its acquisition of lands that had belonged to Germany for centuries. "To put Poland in such borders was to make it perforce a Russian protectorate, whether its government was Communist or not." There was logic in such a conclusion; yet this was not what happened.

Now I come to George Kennan's unexpected and extraordinary work: his two books about the origins of the First World War in Europe* — more exactly, about the origins of the Franco-Russian alliance, 1875 to 1894. His reasons for this work are easy to ascertain. Throughout his life, and in many of his writings and addresses, he insisted that the greatest catastrophe of the twentieth century was the outbreak of the First World War, with its myriad disastrous consequences, of which the Russian revolution was one. His qualifications for such a detailed diplomatic history are obvious too. He had been a diplomatist, a student of international relations and their history; drawing on such potential assets he had become an accomplished historian. In the Introduction of the first volume, *The Decline of Bismarck's European Order: Franco-Russian Relations, 1875–1890,* he wrote that he was aware of "the hackneyed subject of the origins of the First World War" to which he wanted to contribute something like "a micro-history."

---

*They were preceded by a small book, *The Marquis de Custine and His Russia in 1839,* Princeton, 1971.

More than a micro-history that was. Amazing, again, are his energy, assiduity, imagination. He began reading, researching, planning, writing this first volume at the age of seventy, finishing the second before eighty. During that time he wrote more than a dozen articles and book reviews and two other books.* It seems that the writing of these volumes took him about four years each. In order to find sources — of so many kinds — in archives and libraries, some of them remote and forlorn, he traveled to Copenhagen, Vienna, Brussels, Bonn, Moscow, Helsinki, and Paris. There he spent long months, residing in a small hotel on the rue de Bourgogne, issuing therefrom to the library of the Quai d'Orsay, which was close, and to the Bibliothèque Nationale (as well as to the dust-laden newspaper archives of *Le Figaro*), which was not. (Apart from these journeys for research during these years, he also traveled to Leningrad, the Black Sea, India, China, Germany, southwest Africa, Norway, writing his impressions of them in innumerable pages of his diary.) Among other matters he took time and effort to look at the small château in the Dordogne where General Obruchev, the prime planner of the Russian-French alliance, lived with his French wife in the summers of the 1890s, talking with General Boisdeffre, his French counterpart; and, later, the forsaken grave of the Russian foreign minister, Giers, whose prudence and honesty Kennan admired. That château he could find; that grave he could not.

So here was this American, born in the Middle West, who had

---

* *The Cloud of Danger: Certain Realities of American Foreign Policy,* Boston, 1977; and *The Nuclear Delusion,* New York, 1983, the latter a collection of addresses, articles, interviews.

at least three advantages over many other historians, Americans as well as European ones. One was his near-perfect knowledge of Russian and German and French. Another was his knowledge of the international history of nineteenth-century Europe. The third, and probably most important, was his incisive knowledge of the details and conditions and circumstances not only of foreign ministries and embassies but of the societies and the imperial courts of Russia and Germany — and thus of the men and women who lived and wrote and talked there. He was not, and never aspired to be, a man of the world; but what he did not know of the characters of the aristocratic and haut-bourgeois lives of that period remains hardly worth knowing. It is his rendition of these societies and their atmosphere that make these volumes superior to the otherwise serious reconstructions of diplomatic history before the First World War, such as William Langer's of Harvard.*

Here and there — and especially in the first volume — one may detect his tendency to unravel almost every small thread, an inclination to include everything, even if but marginally relevant to his subject. Such was his extensive treatment of the Bulgarian crises of 1885–86, occupying more than one hundred pages; and later an analysis of the provenance of the forged "Ferdinand documents" that he found important enough to dissect and describe in a separate scholarly article.† There was, too, his fascination

---

* Kennan of course relied on many of the important historical works about his topic; he acknowledged them emphatically — for example, Professor Pieter Jakobs's *Das Werden der französisch-russischen Zweibundes, 1890–1894,* Wiesbaden, 1968.
† Published in the German journal *Jahrbücher für die Geschichte Osteuropas,* 1978, pp. 321ff.

with an interloper in diplomacy, the extraordinary and intriguing figure of Elie Cyon.

However—questions may be raised not about Kennan's details but about what may be seen as the general inclination of his narrative account. His marshaling of the evidence of the origins of and of the complicated negotiations leading up to the alliance in 1894 may not be superseded. Historians will also agree that in 1890 Bismarck's departure from the command of the German ship of state was a great and grave change, with many consequences. Respect for Bismarck's statesmanship is certainly warranted. But in these two books, especially in the first, Kennan's admiration for Bismarck is unstinted. He esteems and defends the German chancellor throughout.* More important: yes, with Bismarck gone, an (in any event, not very stable) European "order" began to wobble: but was the subsequent alliance of France with Russia really as disastrous and fateful as Kennan's very title for his second volume states: *The Fateful Alliance: France, Russia, and the Coming of the First World War*? For the sake of a balance of powers, was not the Franco-Russian alliance an expectable reaction against the then overwhelming German alliance system? In his Epilogue to the second book Kennan wrote "that of the four great powers most immediately affected by the Franco-Russian Alliance—France, Russia, Germany and Austria-Hungary—the only two that had what might be called clear expansionist motives were the two parties of the Alliance—France and Russia." This, too, is arguable.†

* At least in one instance his insight into character is arguable: Bismarck "was in many respects . . . a man of the eighteenth century." Yet did not Bismarck, for example, know very well how to manipulate the press?
† It must not be thought that Kennan was dismissive of the French

Worth noticing are the changed conditions in the publications
of the two volumes — together with indications that their author's intentions may have been changing too. The first volume
was published by Princeton University Press, but the second by
Pantheon Books in New York. (A future biographer must ascertain why.) The very design and typography of the two books
is quite different, the first with the marks of a serious university press, the second less so. There are (very rare in Kennan's
books) many typographical errors in the second. Moreover, the
first volume has a serious and thoughtful Bibliographical Essay,
the second one has not. At the end of the first book the seventy-
four-year-old Kennan wrote: "What followed in the years immediately ahead [of 1890] . . . will make suitable material for a
further volume of this study, always assuming that these common hazards of personal life that attend the completion of most
large undertakings of historical scholarship will permit, by the
grace of Providence, the accomplishment of this one." Yes; Providence allowed — and, if may say so, impelled — Kennan to complete a second volume; but not a third. Four years later, in the
Introduction to *The Fateful Alliance,* we may still read: "A third
part, still to be written, should carry the tale from 1894 down to
the total collapse of the Alliance in the turmoil of the Russian
Revolution. . . . in 1917–1918." Whether Kennan penned this
Introduction at the start or at the end of his work on the second
volume we do not know. But what is remarkable is his plan to
carry the story of that Fateful Alliance not only to 1914 but to

---

throughout. "Of the 470,000 male infants born in France in the year 1890
fully half were fated either to meet an early and painful death in World War I
or to emerge from that bloodbath maimed or otherwise injured."

1917 — as if France's alliance with Russia had led to the Russian revolutions in 1917. And then he chose not to attempt this — with plenty of reasons, of which his advancing age must have been but one.* Many, many things happened with the Franco-Russian alliance and the European balance of power from 1894 to 1914 . . . and beyond. A third volume — unless quite different in structure and composition than the preceding two — could sum that up but not contain all of it.

This is how the very title of *The Fateful Alliance: France, Russia, and the Coming of the First World War* is somewhat misleading. There were other fateful alliances, too; the 1894 one was one, but only one, and not the immediate or even direct factor of the outbreak of the First World War. Still, these two volumes by Kennan deserve to be classed as magisterial. Yet it may be note-worthy that, after having received respectable and complimentary reviews, these are two of Kennan's important books that have not had foreign translations.

4

What were some of the particular qualities of George Kennan's historianship? The assets that he brought to his history writing I summed up briefly earlier. Of course every asset is not merely actual but potential: their possession may be one thing, and their employment another. There are two fundamental elements in his historianship to which I wish now to draw attention.

---

* In 1985, a year after the publication of *The Fateful Alliance,* he returned to ruminate about that alliance after 1894, in his remarks at the Kennan Institute for Advanced Russian Studies, reprinted in a pamphlet in 1986.

The first is that — in one sense, in a rather old-fashioned way — Kennan saw history as literature. But in one sense only: because his works are not tale-telling, they include what is called a scholarly apparatus, references to accumulated materials of sources and scholarly writings about his topics. He would, I think, have agreed that serious history is a compound of art and science. Whether he would agree to my, rather severe, dictum that historians who cannot write well cannot be good historians, I cannot tell. He certainly knew that words are not simply the additions, the clothing of facts but that they are inseparable from the "facts" themselves. There exist one or two articles or lectures of his where he expounded a little on his view of history as a form of literature. Within his histories there are many illustrations of this. His descriptions of places and of their atmospheres are not only the best-written and the most charming portions of his chapters; they are also the most telling ones. Their method is impressionistic, their impulse is romantic, and their result is evocative. There are evidences of his purpose in his own words. Here is one example from his Introduction of *The Decline of Bismarck's European Order:* "It is my hope that this work will serve, in addition to [this] severely scholarly practice, to illuminate . . . and to evoke that ineffable quality of atmosphere without which no era of history can be made real and plausible to those who have not themselves experienced it." His sweeping descriptions of particular societies in particular times, often at the beginning of his different books, are superb. So are, too, his masterly portraits of cityscapes and landscapes, of streets and houses, of frontier villages, of train journeys of a certain time. One has the impression that he chose to include them and to render them tellingly and finely may not only have seemed proper but pleasurable for him. In this respect "le style c'est l'homme" applies to Kennan the historian.

Style is, of course, a reflection. That Kennan was a man of the written word we know. But underneath that were his convictions: that history was more than a social science, because the life of the mind is more than an intellectual function, because human life itself is more than a scientific matter. He saw the moral and religious essence of every human proposition, including the conscious uses of human memory. Thus he may have exemplified the beautiful phrase of his contemporary the French writer Jean Dutourd whom he did not know: "Écrire une histoire c'est transformer un morceau de temps en un morceau d'éternité" — to write a history is to transform a fragment of time into a morsel of foreverness.

# SEVEN

# Philosophy, Religion; Memory; Old Age

I

In 1989 George Kennan was eighty-five years old. His prestige had reached its zenith. The president awarded him the Presidential Medal of Freedom. The head of the Soviet Union had grasped his hand and poured words of gratitude onto him. The Cold War was over. His recognition as "the architect of American foreign policy" during that Cold War was now complete, unchallenged, nearly universal. He took little or no interest in these encomia. He saw something else: that he was man of a century, the twentieth, which was now irremediably past. "I was ten years old in 1914, and eighty-five in 1989," he wrote in the beginning of yet another book, *At a Century's Ending,* that "while each of the last few centuries of European history seemed to have a certain specific character of its own," the twentieth century was a short one, that it began with the First World War that led to the Second that led to the Cold War, lasting thus from 1914 to 1989. He also thought — and said this, more than often, to his family and to some of his friends — that his life had come to its ending too.

He was wrong. Save for expectable vicissitudes (pain in his knees) his body remained by and large unbroken, for another ten years at least. His mind weakened not at all. He wrote two entirely new books, composed and put together two or three others; he wrote a dozen articles and book reviews, gave a few public addresses; he kept writing his diary and letters intermittently. Their quality was as fine in his nineties as it ever was.* He and his wife traveled until the ninety-ninth year of his life, even though he hated air travel. They flew to their small house in Norway every summer. Their domestic life was made easier after their children had insisted and then arranged for them to get domestic help. Their relations with the latter (among them a young Polish woman with an enormous and amiable dog; and then, for many years, a devoted Portuguese couple) were marked by reciprocal affections.

When they came to Princeton in 1950 they were newcomers. Now they were the most honored of its inhabitants. Their ochre-colored house on a quiet residential street, with their garden behind it, was a modest mansion, solidly American in construction and in the arrangement of its rooms, yet its interiors breathed a subtle patrician atmosphere that would befit a cozy dwelling somewhere in northern Europe, and not only because that (and Russia) was the provenance of a few of its furnishings and

---

* So was, amazingly, his handwriting: careful, precise, handsome and legible till the end.

pictures. Most of George's library and work room was on the second floor. He had no computer (later in those years a fax machine was put in, but one managed only by his now part-time secretary). He would now visit his office at the Institute (where he had become emeritus after he reached seventy) several days a week until almost his ninety-eighth year, in 2001. The eleventh of September that year was his and Annelise's seventieth wedding anniversary, celebrated by their children.

2

He kept watching the course of great events throughout, concerned for his country, compelled enough to rush into writing at one or another instance. In 1988 he wrote in a letter: "What you call 'a split-mindedness' runs through the entire fabric of American politics and attitudes towards the Soviet Union. One great part of the United States government professes to be seeking peace with Moscow, another great part of it — the CIA and the Pentagon — appears to live and act on the assumption that we are either at war with Russia or are about to be. Both of these attitudes have their domestic cliques and constituencies — and our good president [Ronald Reagan then], anxious to retain the support of both of them, wages peace, demonstratively, out of one pocket, and war, clandestinely, out of the other. Hence — his split mind." Earlier, in an address to Grinnell College in Iowa, he called "for a greater restraint than we have shown in recent decades in involving ourselves in complex situations far from our shores. And it is a plea to bear in mind that in the interactions of peoples, just as in the interactions of individuals, the power of example is far greater than the power of precept; and that the example offered to the world at this moment by the United States of America is far from being what it could be and ought to be."* He took it upon himself to write long and thoughtful book reviews, for instance of the autobiography of Andrei Gromyko, and of his friend Robert Tucker's biography of Stalin, suggesting his occasional disagreements, and urging the latter to go on beyond 1939 and write of the last fourteen years of Stalin's life.

In 1989 portions of his travel diaries were printed under the unassuming title *Sketches from a Life.* He had put these together reluctantly, after the urging of a close friend who had admired portions of the diaries that Kennan had shown or sent him occasionally. Future Americans who, besides their respect for his political sagacity, discover the high literary value of his writing may see this as one of his finest books, and a stimulus to read more of Kennan (somewhat like Tocqueville's privately written and late-published *Souvenirs,* which might be the best introduction for those who then would wish to read more of Tocqueville). Someday a very much larger selection of George Kennan's diaries and letters ought to be judiciously selected, edited, and printed in an impressive volume.

But after the publication of *Sketches from a Life* another, long

---

* (On 1 February 1984.) He continued: "Let us present the world outside our borders the face of a country that has learned to cope with crime and poverty and corruption, with drugs and pornography—let us prove ourselves capable of taking the great revolution of electronic communications in which we are all today embraced and turning it to the intellectual and spiritual elevation of our people in place of the enervation and debilitation and abuse of the intellect that television now so often inflicts upon them. Let us do these things, and others like them, and we will not need 27,000 nuclear warheads and a military budget of over $250 billion to make the influence of America felt in the world beyond our borders."

pregnant, impulse started to move his mind and hand: a *summa* of his personal and political philosophy that he thought was long overdue, and that now must be written, near the end of his life. In September 1991 he wrote in a letter: "I entered this task, some months ago, light-heartedly and almost casually. The farther I go with it the more sobered and impressed with what I have taken upon myself . . . " This turned out to be *Around a Cragged Hill: A Personal and Political Philosophy,* published by W. W. Norton in 1993.

"I have taken the high ground, avoiding all detailed preoccupations with current problems," he wrote in his Foreword, drafted after the composition of the main text of the work. It was not one of his best books. George Kennan had an extraordinary mind; but he was not a philosopher.* That "but" is not a caveat: a great mind is not necessarily a philosopher; consider only Samuel Johnson, for one example. Kennan was deeply religious, but this is not the place to summarize what he wrote about his personal philosophy in this book. His God-belief and his belief of man's original sinfulness are evident in its pages, though I, for one, find a kind of transcendentalism in one of its most telling paragraphs, recording his "own conviction that the soul has an existence wholly separate from the body." But the main problems with *Around the Cragged Hill* are not his religious or philosophical ruminations. They are results of his concerns with the state. It is his conclusion, in the last chapter of this book, to which he devoted so much thought and effort. There he proposes a Council of State, to be composed of persons of high distinction, appointed by the president of the United States, to advise in setting

---

* "Abstraction has never been my dish," he wrote in a footnote.

the course of the ship of state on the highest level. Throughout his life Kennan struggled with the, surely for him, inevitable shortcomings of popular democracy. We have seen that in the 1930s he had a sympathetic regard for certain authoritarian regimes; and that, in 1938, he started to write a book about the, to him, unavoidable correction of popular and parliamentary government. That book he never finished; fortunately enough, he abandoned it. But somehow, more than fifty years later, he now returned to such preoccupations with what he considered a reasonable and practical proposal. Yet reasonable and/or practical it was not. (Just think of appointees of George W. Bush: whom would such a president appoint to a Council of State, and why?)

More valuable and more enduring was *At a Century's Ending,* published in 1996, a volume with impressive and rich contents, though little noticed at the time. Again this was more than a usual collection of articles; its pieces fit together very well; they also included one last essay that had not been published before. The first sentence of one article (first printed in 1992 in the op-ed section of the *New York Times,* whose editors gave it the title "Republicans Won the Cold War?") read: "The suggestion that any American administration had the power to influence decisively the course of a tremendous political upheaval, in another great country on another side of the globe is intrinsically silly and childish." The last sentence read: "That [the Cold War] itself should now be formally ended is a fit occasion for satisfaction, but also for sober reexamination of the part we took in its origin and in its long continuation. It is not a fit occasion for pretending that the end of it was a great triumph for anyone, and particularly one for which any American political party could properly claim credit." But he was — with plenty of reasons — as disheartened by the foreign policy of the Democratic Clinton's administration as with the preceding Republican one. He chose to include in this book an excerpt from his diary on 9 December 1992: "I have left it unedited, exactly as it was then written,"* about American troops sent to Somalia. "The dispatch of American armed forces to a seat of operations in a place far from our own shores, and this for what is actually a major police action in another country and in a situation where no defensible American interest is involved — this, obviously, is something that the Founding Fathers never envisaged or would ever have approved. If this is in the American tradition, then it is a very recent tradition, and one quite out of accord with the general assumptions that have governed American public life for most of the last two hundred years." In the last, previously unpublished, concluding essay of this book, "The New Russia as a Neighbor," he wrote, ever so wisely: "That Russia will ever achieve 'democracy,' in the sense of political, social, and economic institutions similar to our own, is not to be expected. And even if Russian forms of self-government should differ significantly from our own, it is not to be postulated that this would be entirely a bad thing. Our own models, as most of us would agree, are not at all that perfect. And there will continue to be ups and downs in our relationship with Russia, as there are today."

Soon after the publication of *At a Century's Ending* President Clinton and his secretary of state and the Pentagon chose to extend the North Atlantic Treaty Organization to a number of eastern European states, many of them bordering Russia, some

---

* It was reprinted in the *New York Times* nine months later (30 September 1993).

of them former parts of the Soviet Union itself. Kennan thought and wrote (again in the op-ed page of the *New York Times*) that this thoughtless expansion of a "North Atlantic" alliance might be the most disastrous mistake of American foreign policy in recent decades. Few people read his words. His solitary warning was not heard.

Yes: it was too late, and — perhaps — too late in his life. On the American intellectual canopy he was now one fading star. Where in a world where celebrity had replaced society, where the cultivation of publicity was even more important than the search for popularity, did he belong? And was that, really, a new condition? Think where, for three decades or more before 1997, apart from his books, his most important writings had appeared: in the *New York Review of Books,* in the *New Yorker,* or on the op-ed pages of the *New York Times.* A few — very few — thousands of people may have read them but not more. And during those thirty or more years a landslide, if not a revolution, had taken place in the United States. In 1950 there was not a single American political or public figure who would have called himself A Conservative. Three decades later more Americans designated themselves as conservatives than liberals, and presidents found it politic and proper to designate themselves thus. Yet no conservative journal or newspaper, and few if any "conservative" politicians paid even the slightest of notices to George Kennan; "conservative" intellectuals attacked his writings on selected occasions. Nor must it be thought that American liberal "opinion" was influenced by him in any significant measure. There was much in his thinking and analyses and advocacies that was not "liberal" (and certainly not "progressive"). Liberal public writers and liberal academics sensed this, sometimes uneasily, sometimes not. He was, by and large, ignored. That was not the result of political or intellectual conspiracy. It was, rather, the result of not an incapacity but an unwillingness to think of some things worth thinking about. A conscience of America? But isn't the voice of a conscience inescapably a lonely voice?

3

Slowly, gradually now his mind moved from philosophy and statecraft to concentrate on religion and memory. He was born Presbyterian, and he paid a generous tribute to his Presbyterian ancestors in yet one more book he would write; but that midwestern and middle-class religion, with remnants of belief in predestination (and with its anti-Catholicism), never attracted him. Early in life he found that he agreed with the admonition of another former midwesterner, Reinhold Niebuhr: "The Gospel cannot be preached with truth and power if it does not challenge the pretensions and pride, not only of intellectuals, but of nations, cultures, civilizations, economic and political systems. The good fortune of America and its power place it under the most grievous temptations to self-adulation." During his life his respect for the Roman Catholic Church grew. Sometime in the 1970s he was inclined to approach the Catholic Church, perhaps with the help of a priest. In the chapter "Faith" in *Around the Cragged Hill* he wrote: "For the Roman Catholic Church I have feelings (at this point some of my ancestors will turn over in their graves) of high respect and, in some instances, admiration."*

---

* In a letter to a young historian, Anders Stephanson, in 1993 he wrote: "What I said . . . understates, if anything, my respect for [that] great

Thereafter he found solace and comfort in the Episcopal Church, descendant of the Church of England that he once, with a charming, if imprecise, phrase called "a partially rebellious child" of the Roman Catholic one.

It is more than customary, it is expectable for a man growing old to think more and more about his ancestors. That worthy effort to extend one's memory (for this is what that amounts to) was fortified and activated by Kennan's acute historical sense. In the summer of 1993 he journeyed to Scotland, to the town of Dumfries, to search for and see and read something of the place wherefrom his Kennan ancestors had gone to the New World. He found revealing files and some archival materials and the marked grave of at least one Kennan. After his return to Princeton he felt compelled to write a seven-page, tightly typed letter to his "Siblings, Children, Grandchildren and Friends."* During the next few years, amid, as we have seen, many other self-imposed tasks, he traveled and followed his researches in various Massachusetts and New York historical societies and libraries, with what he found were precious results.†

The result was his last book, written in the ninety-seventh year of his life, well done sufficiently to be produced and published by

---

institution . . . . I have been impressed (without always sharing the various points of departure) with such evidences of European-Catholic thinking as have from time to time come to my attention."

* "All these things I did, stumbling about on my stick under the anxious supervision of Annelise and a very nice Irish driver we had hired for the week."

† His acknowledgments were directed especially to the librarians of these different American societies: "As one who regards its library culture as probably the greatest of this country's contributions to world culture, help from that quarter has had a special meaning to me."

his trade publisher, Norton, with the title *An American Family: The Kennans, the First Three Generations,* in 2000. The decision of Norton's editors to publish such a book involved more than their respect (and indebtedness) to Kennan, since *An American Family: The Kennans* is much more than a genealogy. It has all the signs of that curious combination of serious restraint and nervous energy typical of his writing. His research was, of course, unexceptionable. But Kennan not only traced but described — depending on the concreteness of evidence but also inspired by the energy of his imagination — the lives of his ancestors who came from Scotland to Massachusetts and then moved to upper New York State and in the end to Wisconsin. As usual, his best portraits are not only of people but also of places. There is, too, his theme that, no matter how westward the destiny of the Kennans took them, they brought with themselves, as did other millions of Americans who were former New Englanders, significant traits and traditions from that provenance. He paid especial homage (that, again, was typical of him) to the honest and devoted women who were anchors or pillars in the families of his ancestors, even as he found it proper to state his limitations, since most of his material dealt with the male Kennan line, not the female one.

Before writing this substantial book he had composed and privately printed a smaller version of it, distributed among his family and a few friends. What then helped and stimulated *An American Family* was the genealogy written and published by his grandfather Thomas Lathrop Kennan in 1907, who was the first highly respected urban descendant of the Kennans. Yet George Kennan's history of the family stops about 1840, well before his grandfather. There is nothing about his grandfather's youth and of his rather successful move to and career in Milwaukee. There is some evidence elsewhere that he did not particularly admire this grandfather. For whatever reasons, in this instance, too, he chose to stop before completing the story.

The book was published in October 2000. A few weeks later he wrote a sixteen-page (again closely typed) letter to his daughter Joan about his own faith. He read and reread the Gospels; for a while he thought about what he saw as the contrast between the teachings of Jesus and those of St. Paul — yet another symptom of the vitality of his mind. That began — slowly and intermittently — to weaken in the one hundredth year of his life. He still wrote or dictated letters as late as the first months of 2003. He lived on, preoccupied with the destiny of his nation. He was appalled by the propagation of America's hegemony over the world. He once said about President George W. Bush that he was "profoundly shallow." In a long letter to his nephew and literary executor in February 2003 he saw what was coming.*

---

* "I am finishing this letter on the morning when, according to the press, the United Nations Security Council (weeping over the absence of the French) is supposed to take some action giving sanction to an early attack, almost exclusively by ourselves, on the present regime of Iraq. There is now not the slightest reason to doubt that this action will be undertaken at the earliest day, probably some three weeks off, when all the military preparations are complete. What this is doing has already acted like a burning match to dynamite for the American media, particularly television, which immerses itself delightedly in what it already perceives as a new war. I take an extremely dark view of all this — see it, in fact, the beginning of the end of anything like a normal life for all the rest of us. Too pessimistic? No doubt, no doubt. I know that I am inclined that way, but that is the way I see things, and I cannot contrive to see them any differently. What is being done to our country today is surely something from which we will never be able to restore the sort of a country you and I have known." He sent me a

His last letters were dictated in September 2003. The sixteenth of February in 2004 was his one hundredth birthday. Princeton University assembled a George F. Kennan Centennial conference that he could no longer attend. He was bedridden by then.* A catastrophe befell the Kennans that summer. Annelise fell and broke her hip. He was bereft of her presence for long weeks. Her courage and vitality were such that she recovered somewhat, though shrunken and bent. On a darkening winter afternoon I came to see them in their upstairs bedroom. His head, resting on a pillow, now had a kind of skeletal beauty; he could speak only little, forcing out a few words with increasing difficulty; near the foot of his bed she sat huddled in a wheelchair at a table, uttering a few sensible words, not many. I went out, crushed with sadness; and then Pamela, my wife-to-become, soothed me quietly: "They were together for so long; they are together now; in the same room; aware of each other; still alive."

Save for these last sentences this is not the memoir of a friend but the work of a historian.

He died on 17 March 2005, one year, one month, one day after his one hundredth birthday.

His obituaries recorded his many achievements adequately, often with the praise that was his due. There was a sense of respectful distance in some of them, a sense that George Kennan was part of a now irretrievable past. That is not untrue; and yet he was (and remains) A Man for All Seasons, a triumph of char-

---

copy of this letter and asked me to have it destroyed. For the first and last time I chose not to obey him.

* The day before he was carried to the Institute, where he was able to say a few words to the assembly honoring him.

acter, a man of principles more than of ideas. He had his prejudices, and some of them were odd ones; but he could recognize
them looking into his own mental mirror; and, more, there was
such goodness, such compassion, such charity in his heart that
were sufficient for his mind to correct them. How fortunate was
this country from whose midst such a mind, and such character
could arise! How ignorant or, rather, wasteful were the people
who ignored or misunderstood him! He was not to meant to be
a protagonist of his times; but an American kind of greatness
applies to him as it was applied to another American of whom
someone said, more than 140 years ago, after his death: *Now he
belongs to the ages.*

# Appendix: Two Finest Hours

*4 December 1950: Kennan's Letter to Dean Acheson*

The circumstances of this are recounted on pages 111–12. The Chinese have entered the war in Korea. The American army there retreats in bitter weather. High officials at the Department of State think that the Russians (who have not entered Korea) might help to bring about a cease-fire.

Kennan, retired, is at his farm. His friend Bohlen telephones him from Paris. He ought to go to Washington to advise people there of what can be expected from Russia. Kennan arrives on a day of gloom and doom. He says that to request anything from Russia now would be wholly wrong. One does not approach Russians at a time of weakness and trouble. Late that afternoon he sees the secretary of state, who is worn down. Suddenly Acheson asks Kennan to come home with him. They have dinner in a largely empty house (only Mrs. Acheson is at home). They talk late into the night. Next morning Kennan rises early. His mind is agitated but clear. He writes the following letter in longhand, and puts it on Acheson's desk first thing in the morning.

◆ ◆ ◆

Dear Mr. Secretary:

There is one thing I should like to say in continuation of our discussion of yesterday evening.

In international, as in private, life what counts most is not really what happens to someone but how he bears what happens to him. For this reason almost everything depends from here on out on the manner in which we Americans bear what is unquestionably a major failure and disaster to our national fortunes. If we accept it with candor, with dignity, with a resolve to absorb its lessons and to make it good by redoubled and determined effort — starting all over again, if necessary, along the pattern of Pearl Harbor — we need lose neither our self-confidence nor our allies nor our power for bargaining, eventually, with the Russians. But if we try to conceal from our own people or from our allies the full measure of our misfortune, or permit ourselves to seek relief in any reactions of bluster or petulance or hysteria, we can easily find this crisis resolving itself into an irreparable deterioration of our world position — and of our confidence in ourselves.

◆ ◆ ◆

Both Acheson and Kennan found it proper to include the entirety of this letter in their respective memoirs.

### 15 May 1953: Kennan's Speech at the University of Notre Dame

The time of this speech is significant. Kennan spoke when Senator Joseph McCarthy's power and influence were at their highest. President Eisenhower chose not to oppose McCarthy in public. His secretary of the army and other members of the cabinet, as well as most senators and congressmen, thought it best to show that they agreed with McCarthy's anticommunist purposes and with some of his means. Polls, whatever their value, reported that about fifty percent of the American people agreed with McCarthy. Kennan was still one month away from his official and final retirement. He still had a desk somewhere in John Foster Dulles's State Department.

◆ ◆ ◆

I find it difficult to begin these remarks without telling you how much it means to me to be here, in my native Middle West, and yet in just such a setting and for just such an occasion. One is always sensitive about one's native region, as one is about one's own family; and in the return to it one looks at it with eyes at once eagerly wistful and ruthlessly critical.

The sense of warmth and reassurance that flows from this occasion means all the more to me because I cannot forget that there are forces at large in our society today that do not inspire me with this same feeling—quite the contrary. These forces are too diffuse to be described by their association with the name of any one man or any one political concept. They have no distinct organizational forms. They are as yet largely matters of the mind and the emotion in large masses of individuals. But they all march, in one way or another, under the banner of an alarmed and exercized anti-communism—but an anti-communism of a quite special variety, bearing an air of excited discovery and proprietorship, as though no one had ever known before that there was a communist danger, as though no one had ever thought about it and taken its measure, as though it had all begun about the year 1945 and these people were the first to learn of it.

I have no quarrel to pick with the ostensible purposes of the people in whom these forces are manifest. Surely, many of them are sincere. Surely, many of them are good people. Surely, many of them have come to these views under real provocation and out of real bewilderment. But I have the deepest misgivings about the direction and effects of their efforts. In general, I feel that what they are doing is unwise and unfortunate, and I am against it. They distort and exaggerate the dimensions of the problem with which they profess to deal. They confuse internal and external aspects of the communist threat. They insist on portraying as contemporary realities things that had their actuality years ago. They insist on ascribing to the workings of domestic communism evils and frustrations which, in so far as they were not part of the normal and unavoidable burden of complexity in our life, were the product of our behavior generally as a nation, and should today be the subject of humble and contrite soul-searching on the part of all of us, in a spirit of brotherhood and community, rather than of frantic and bitter recrimination. And having thus incorrectly stated the problem, it is no wonder that these people consistently find the wrong answers. They tell us to remove our eyes from the constructive and positive purposes and to pursue with fanaticism the negative and vindictive ones. They sow timidity where there should be boldness; fear where there should be serenity; suspicion where there should be confidence and generosity. In this way they impel us — in the name of our salvation from the dangers of communism — to many of the habits of thought and action which our Soviet adversaries, I am sure, would most like to see us adopt and which they have tried unsuccessfully over a period of some 35 years to graft upon us through the operations of their communist party.

I would not mention these things if I felt that they were only my personal concern and had no relation to the undertaking which we have gathered today to celebrate. But I fear that there is here a serious relevance which we cannot ignore.

Thanks to the vision of wise and generous people, this University is now adding one more important unit to the number of those facilities in our country in which men can cultivate their own understanding, and extend the boundaries of knowledge, in the field of arts and letters. Certainly there could be no finer undertaking, and none more needed. But I feel that this undertaking, too, will have to deal at some point with the forces I have just described — that by entering upon this undertaking you will eventually find that these forces will be your concern just as they have already become the concern of some of us who have walked in other branches of life.

I feel this first of all because these forces are narrowly exclusive in their approach to our world position, and carry this exclusiveness vigorously into the field of international cultural exchanges. They tend to stifle the interchange of cultural impulses that is vital to the progress of the intellectual and artistic life of our people. The people in question seem to feel either that cultural values are not important at all or that America has reached the apex of cultural achievement and no longer needs in any serious way the stimulus of normal contact with other peoples in the field of arts and letters. They look with suspicion both on the sources of intellectual and artistic activity in this country and on impulses of this nature coming to us from abroad. The remote pasts of foreign artists and scholars are anxiously scanned before they are permitted to enter our land, and this is done in proceedings so inflexible in concept and offensive in execution that their very existence often constitutes a discouragement to cultural interchange. The personal movements and affairs of great scholars and artists are thus passed upon and controlled by people who have no inkling of understanding for the creative work these same scholars and artists perform. In this way, we begin to draw about ourselves a cultural curtain similar in some respects to the iron curtain of our adversaries. In doing so, we tend to inflict upon ourselves a species of cultural isolation and provincialism wholly out of accord with the traditions of our nation and destined, if unchecked, to bring to our intellectual and artistic life the same sort of sterility from which the cultural world of our communist adversaries is already suffering.

A second reason why I think you will have to concern yourselves with the forces to which I have pointed is that within the framework of our society, as in its relations to external environment, the tendency of these forces is exclusive and intolerant — quick to reject, slow to receive, intent on discovering what ought *not* to be rather than what *ought* to be. They claim the right to define a certain area of our national life and cultural output as beyond the bounds of righteous approval. This definition is never effected by law or by constituted authority; it is effected by vague insinuation and suggestion. And the circle, as I say, tends to grow constantly narrower. One has the impression that if uncountered, these people would eventually narrow the area of political and cultural respectability to a point where it included only themselves, the excited accusers, and excluded everything and everybody not embraced in the profession of denunciation.

I recall reading recently, twice in one day, the words of individuals who proclaimed that if certain other people did not get up and join actively in the denunciation of communists or communism, they would thereby themselves be suspect. What sort of arrogance is this? Every one of us has his civic obligations. Every one of us has his moral obligations to the principles of loyalty and decency. I am not condoning any one for forgetting these obligations. But to go beyond this — to say that it is not enough to be a law-abiding citizen — to say that we all have some obligation to get up and make statements of this tenor or that with respect to other individuals, or else submit to being classified as suspect in the eyes of our fellow citizens — to assert this is to establish a new species of public ritual, to arrogate to one's individual self the powers of the spiritual and temporal law-giver, to make the definition of social conduct a matter of fear in the face of vague and irregular forces, rather than a matter of confidence in the protecting discipline of conscience and the law.

I would know of no moral or political authority for this sort of thing. I tremble when I see this attempt to make a semi-religious cult out of emotional-political currents of the moment, and particularly when I note that these currents are ones exclusively negative in nature, de-signed to appeal only to men's capacity for hatred and fear, never to their capacity for forgiveness and charity and understanding. I have lived more than ten years of my life in totalitarian countries. I know where this sort of thing leads. I know it to be the most shocking and cynical disservice one can do to the credulity and to the spiritual equilibrium of one's fellowmen.

And this sort of thing cannot fail to have its effect on the liberal arts, for it is associated with two things that stand in deepest conflict to the development of mind and spirit: with a crass materialism and anti-intellectualism on the one hand, and with a marked tendency toward standardization and conformity on the other.

In these forces I have spoken about, it seems to me that I detect a conscious rejection and ridicule of intellectual effort and distinction. They come together here with a deep-seated weakness in the American character: a certain shy self-consciousness that tends to deny interests other than those of business, sport, or war. There is a powerful strain of our American cast of mind that has little use for the artist or the writer, and professes to see in the pursuits of such people a lack of virility — as though virility could not find expression in the creation of beauty, as though Michaelangelo had never wielded his brush, as though Dante had never taken up his pen, as though the plays of Shakespeare were lacking in manliness. The bearers of this neo-materialism seem, indeed, to have a strange self-consciousness about the subject of virility — a strange need to emphasize and demonstrate it by exhibitions of taciturnity, callousness, and physical aggressiveness — as though there were some anxiety lest, in the absence of these exhibitions, it might be found wanting. What weakness is it in us Americans that so often makes us embarrassed or afraid to indulge the gentle impulse, to seek the finer and rarer flavor, to admit frankly and without stammering apologies to an appreciation for the wonder of the poet's word and the miracle of the artist's brush, for all the beauty, in short, that has been recorded in the images of word and line created by the hands of men in past ages? What is it that makes us fear to acknowledge the greatness of other lands, or of other times, to shun the subtle and the unfamiliar? What is it that causes us to huddle together, herdlike, in tastes and enthusiasms that represent only the common denominator of popular acquiescence rather than to show ourselves receptive to the tremendous flights of creative imagination of which the individual mind has shown itself capable? Is it that we are forgetful of the true sources of our moral strength, afraid of ourselves, afraid to look into the chaos of our own breasts, afraid of the bright, penetrating light of the great teachers?

This fear of the untypical, this quest for security within the walls of secular uniformity — these are traits of our national character we would do well to beware of and to examine for their origins. They receive much encouragement these days, much automatic and unintended encouragement, by virtue of the growing standardization of the cultural and, in many respects, the educational influences to which our people are being subjected. The immense impact of commercial advertising and the mass media on our lives is — let us make no mistake about it — an impact that tends to encourage passivity, to encourage acquiescence and uniformity, to place handicaps on individual contemplativeness and creativeness.

It may not seem to many of us too dangerous that we should all live, dress, eat, hear, and read substantially alike. But we forget how easily this uniformity of thought and habit can be exploited, when the will to exploit it is there. We forget how easily it can slip over into the domination of our spiritual and political lives by self-appointed custodians who contrive to set themselves at the head of popular emotional currents.

There is a real and urgent danger here for anyone who values the right to differ from others in any manner whatsoever, be it in his interests or his associations or his faith. There is no greater mistake we of this generation can make than to imagine that the tendencies which in other countries have led to the nightmare of totalitarianism will, as they appear in our own midst, politely pause — out of some delicate respect for American tradition — at the point where they would begin to affect our independence of mind and belief. The forces of intolerance and political demagoguery are greedy forces, and unrestrained. There is no limit to their ambitions or their impudence. They contain within themselves no mechanism of self-control. Like the ills of Pandora's box, once released, they can be stopped only by forces external to themselves.

It is for these reasons that I feel that you, in setting up at this time within this great academic community a center for liberal arts, are taking upon yourselves a great, though honorable, burden. You are going to have to swim against the tide of many of the things I have been talking about. You are frequently going to find arrayed against you, whether by intent or otherwise, the materialists, the anti-intellectuals, the chauvinists of all sizes and descriptions, the protagonists of violence and suspicion and intolerance, the people who take it upon themselves to delimit the operation of the principle of Christian charity, the people from whose memories there has passed the recollection that in their Father's house there are many mansions. What you do in these walls will often be unsettling and displeasing to such people. They will view it with jealousy. You will have to bear their malice and their misrepresentation. But, unlike what many of them profess to wish to do to their own chosen enemies, it will be your task not to destroy them but to help in their redemption and remaking, to open their eyes, to demonstrate to them the sterility and hopelessness of negative undertakings, to engender in them an awareness of the real glories and the real horizons of the human spirit.

In this lies both the duty and the opportunity of the devotees of the liberal arts within our contemporary American civilization. It lies with them to combat the standardization of our day: to teach people to accept the great richness of the human mind and fantasy — to welcome it and to rejoice in it, happy that we have not been condemned by Nature to a joyless monotony of the creative faculty, happy that there are so many marvelous ways in which the longings and dreams of men can find expression. It lies with the devotees of the liberal arts to combat the materialism of our time: to teach us how to ride to work in a motor vehicle and absorb the canned music of the advertisers without forgetting that there is also a music of the spheres, to force us to remember that all the manifestations of our material prowess, impressive as they seem, are nevertheless only impermanent auxiliaries to our existence — that the only permanent thing behind them all is still the naked, vulnerable, human soul, the scene of the age-old battle between good and evil, assailed with weakness and imperfections, always in need of help and support, and yet sometimes capable of such breathtaking impulses of faith and creative imagination.

Finally, it lies with the devotees of the liberal arts to combat the forces of intolerance in our society: to convince people that these forces are incompatible with the flowering of the human spirit, to remember that the ultimate judgments of good and evil are not ours to make: that the wrath of man against his fellow man must always be tempered by the recollection of his weakness and fallibility and by the example of forgiveness and redemption which is the essence of his Christian heritage.

I have tried to give you in these words a picture of the role of the liberal arts institution as I see it, and of its relation to the problems of our American civilization at this time. I assign to it in my thoughts, as you see, a duty and a function that could hardly be more important. To those of you who are going to participate in the direction of this institution, and to those who are going to work within its sheltering and inspiring walls, I can only say that you have the deepest good wishes and the bated hopes of all of us who wish to see preserved the great qualities by which this nation has thus far been distinguished: its tolerance, its good nature, its decency, its health of spirit. May your accomplishments be worthy of your opportunities. May they give fruition to the excellent impulses that have made possible this beginning.

# Suggestions for Further Research

This book is not an extensive biography of George Kennan but a study of his character — inevitably biographical and chronological as this is. Throughout its pages I have made several suggestions of this or that topic or question that future biographers or students of Kennan ought to explore. I shall not repeat them here.*

The daunting problem is the, again earlier mentioned, tremendous amount of Kennan's literary heritage, much larger than what could be otherwise expected from a man of the written word. He may have been the last American who left such an immense trove behind. (Keep in mind, too, that there is not the slightest evidence that he wrote with an eye to posterity.) The extent of his written residue is such that a wholly complete bibliography, including both his published and unpublished papers, may not be possible. Added to the excellent and commend-

---

*Let me add that perhaps one group of important subjects to be explored further exists within Kennan's various writings, especially diaries and letters, in and about Germany, especially before, during, and after his stationing there in 1927, 1928–31, and 1939–41.

able bibliography compiled by Laurel E. Franklin, *George F. Kennan: An Annotated Bibliography,* Greenwood Press, Westport, Conn., 1997, there are still more Kennan books, articles, publications, diaries in the years 1996 to 2003. We probably cannot expect a complete list of foreign translations of his books and of his other writings, and of studies and dissertations written about him in countries beyond the United States. There is no doubt that their number will grow.

A large quantity of his papers are deposited in the Seely G. Mudd Manuscript Library of the Princeton University Libraries, properly cared for, and with a very valuable finding aid, referring to various boxes and their numbers. Kennan transferred most of his papers to Mudd in 1970, when he became emeritus at the Institute. This great collection even includes a few drafts of letters that he decided not to send. Yet it mostly includes papers from the years 1925 to 1970; it includes private papers still not open for research; it does not include all of his diaries (which he intermittently kept from 1923 to 1999!) or all of his correspondence. His personal papers were kept in his office; they are now in his family's possession; we may hope that they will be deposited in Mudd sooner or later. His correspondence is overwhelming. He kept copies of some of his letters; of others (especially handwritten ones) he of course did not. There must be thousands of his letters kept and treasured by their recipients all over the United States and Britain and Europe. To this writer alone he wrote about two hundred letters, during fifty-one years, 1952 to 2003.

# Index

# Index